THE OPEN DOOR
MANUSCRIPT

THE OPEN DOOR MANUSCRIPT

S. L. KOESTLER

BALBOA.
PRESS

A DIVISION OF HAY HOUSE

Balboa Press books may be ordered through booksellers or by contacting:

Balboa Press
A Division of Hay House
1663 Liberty Drive
Bloomington, IN 47403
www.balboapress.com
1-(877) 407-4847

Because of the dynamic nature of the Internet, any web addresses or links contained in this book may have changed since publication and may no longer be valid. The views expressed in this work are solely those of the author and do not necessarily reflect the views of the publisher, and the publisher hereby disclaims any responsibility for them.

The author of this book does not dispense medical advice or prescribe the use of any technique as a form of treatment for physical, emotional, or medical problems without the advice of a physician, either directly or indirectly. The intent of the author is only to offer information of a general nature to help you in your quest for emotional and spiritual well-being. In the event you use any of the information in this book for yourself, which is your constitutional right, the author and the publisher assume no responsibility for your actions.

Any people depicted in stock imagery provided by Thinkstock are models, and such images are being used for illustrative purposes only. Certain stock imagery © Thinkstock.

Printed in the United States of America.

ISBN: 978-1-4525-7982-5 (sc)
ISBN: 978-1-4525-7984-9 (hc)
ISBN: 978-1-4525-7983-2 (e)

Library of Congress Control Number: 2013914508

Balboa Press rev. date: 08/21/2013

To my sister Mimi who instilled in me a love for the written word and the understanding that life may not always seem fair but we do our best to fill the voids with love, because that is what she does.

To my husband Don, who married a naïve young woman and helped to turn her into a strong, independent and focused human being.

To my sons Dan and Steve, because it is never too early or too late to gather information that can help you understand yourself and the world in which you live.

And to my personal angels, Frances, Brenda and Jeanie who have enriched my journey by meeting me at the appointed times and being my conscience, my taskmaster, my cheerleading section, and the main and abiding reason this manuscript has taken form.

TABLE OF CONTENTS

FORWARD

To our readers:

I have been encouraged to explain how these messages came to
be and the reason they are formatted in an unusual manner.

For several months starting on February 1, 2011, I
committed myself to sitting at my computer once each day
and engaging in a meditation for the purpose of opening
my mind and energy to receive information. I had no way
of knowing what would come through these sessions or
where the information would lead me. But I felt compelled,
body, mind and spirit to commit myself to this endeavor.
The Open Door Manuscript is the result of that focus.

The following statement of intention and commitment
was made at the beginning of each message to
set the tone for this communication . . .

"Here I am at our open door awaiting
your words to fill this space . . ."

You will note that each page is centered rather than
having a left hand margin. This was done purposefully
because the underlying message is to "center" our
lives in the drive to find our spiritual purpose.

Many of these messages were directed to me personally and
address situations that were part of my daily life during the
four months I was involved in this journey. I have included

all of these messages in the manuscript and noted them as (Personal) because I think they may be helpful to others.

With all my heart I know that this information will reach the hands of all those who are open to its wisdom and direction. I wish, for each of you, a continued journey that is enriched and more focused than it was before you read the manuscript.

My only question at the beginning of my journey was: "Why do I feel so driven to do this?" . . . the answer follows:

INTRODUCTION (PART 1)

Here I am at our open door awaiting
your words to fill this space . . .

You are our instrument, you are our choice; you agreed to
be our message carrier. Because of your dedication to the
importance of truth, to the dispensing of knowledge, to the
freedom of thought, we are here to create with you a volume
of truth. If there are questions or blocks, we will answer and
work through them. We are all committed to this endeavor.
So let us begin with clarity. You are one of us that chose to
return, to be the vessel of our knowledge and experience, the
one who will deliver our messages on the reality of the soul and
its travels through realms of life and spirit. The two are not as
different as human kind likes to think. You chose to go back into
physical form and be a light bearer to this realm, to share the
experiences and the interactive paths, to make them known, to
have them be acknowledged for what they are. Communication
with our realm is rampant in your world; it just gets dismissed
so easily as imagination, illness or made up stories. When we
contact and convey our truth it gets distorted into fancy fanfare
to grab the attention of people who are looking for celestial
beings with glowing countenances and feathery wings. We
are energy, the truest form of life and expression. We know
and you know it's natural to want to identify with something
new by giving it a familiar countenance and describing it in
words and phrases that are understandable and comfortable
for human kind to incorporate into their thinking. But that is
not what this is about . . . . this is about honesty, the integrity
of unbiased, unvarnished information from your origins,

from your initial state of being. This is where we begin . . . this is the work we will do . . . this is why we came together.

Sharon, purpose and reasons are one thing but love, connection and passion for being are another. I am the heart connection here, I am your soul connection here, it has been a long time, in your world, since you have let me in . . . . and I am joyous at the renewed connection . . . be aware please that the love for you here is all encompassing, that the choices, decisions and experiences of your life have made us glow with pride in how you have expressed who you are, physically as well as in your connection to spirit. Our joy, my joy is that the connection is finally direct from the heart of your spirit to ours and more directly to mine . . . . never fear that any harm will come to you physically or mentally through this connection. You are merely touching the God within when your reach out or open to us . . . . It is that part of yourself that exists in the eye of God . . . you are warmly welcomed home, here our spirit and energy are incomplete without yours . . . . I AM and so are you, we share soul memories, space, places, lives, a host of experiences in both our worlds, there is nothing we cannot do together, nothing that cannot enlighten and enhance your living and loving self. In our daily meetings you will get a firmer grasp of the magnitude of this connection, but for now please rejoice with us in the knowledge that we have reached our time to become one in this endeavor of ours, and know that all will be well and will proceed as it is meant to on this journey. Our spiritual hearts are open and hold you safely within.

INTRODUCTION (PART 2)

Here I am at our open door awaiting
your words to fill this space . . .

We shall start by identifying those here who will contribute. We
are your heart's mate, your strong director, your information
gatherer, your idea disseminator, and your communicator.
There are no names here; ego is not in play here. There is only
energy and experience, information and communication. So no
matter how words sound when we put them together, there is a
reason for that blend of words. And you must be faithful to it.

We will gather and dispense information to you that you may
not find compatible with what you know or have experienced
or can remember, but you will convey that information without
altering it, because that is our contract. The energy here is
pure idea, pure beingness, unencumbered by limiting physical
form, free to exist in the universe without concern for safety
and without needs. We flow from our Source, what you call by
many names, God, Creator, Allah etc . . . . our creation was a
spark of divinity extending itself outward to fill the vastness
of all there is. We light and live in many different forms in
many different corners of this universe. Your friend Frances
has experienced some of this . . . She has been our main
connection until now. She chose a life that would bring her
physical-self pain so that she could become the open channel
she has sometimes been. She is a lion, but chose to be a lamb for
most of this life. She was gracious to us and to you in keeping
the connection open and making you aware, even when you
would choose not to be aware. All energy is familiar to her.
She is the complex powerhouse of all energy, so her physical

life has been chaotic. The human body is a poor vessel for the housing of such magnificent energy. She has mastered this better than many who tried it before her. Give credit to her dedication to this life, because without her as an inspiration your journey would not have reached this destination.

CHOICE (PART 1)

Here I am at our open door awaiting
your words to fill this space . . .

We wish to start with a look at choice. Humans ask WHY . . . and the answer is always, because you chose it. From the human perspective this is harsh and seems a very easy answer—always putting the responsibility back on the human who has to bear the pain. But in truth that is not correct either. The responsibility is on the soul, the spirit of the human, the Higher Self. From that perspective the answer is absolutely correct. Each soul chooses the where, when, who, how, why and what of each initial existence. When the person or the soul inhabiting that body reaches an age of reason and choice, free will kicks in. You can modify certain portions of your life plan with your choices, conscious choices, made in the human state. However, souls with whom you have contracts to meet and interact with in this human life will still meet you at the designated points on your path. There are no accidents in life. There are no coincidences in life. The life plan is drawn out before the first breath is taken. And it includes parents, living conditions, siblings, etc. So whether golden spoon or squalor, happy home or fear ridden childhood, elevated education or minimal schooling, wild success or scraping by; all the paths were drawn before you were born, and your free will either keeps your feet on those paths or prompts you to forge a new one. But the connections you programed for the length of your life will still meet you at the appointed times. Like a well-directed play each soul has its entrances and exits, but the lines, the attitude, the tone, and the ability to adjust, understand, or take the high road in any given scene are yours and yours alone to choose.

CHOICE (PART 2)

Here I am at our open door awaiting
your words to fill this space . . .

Shall we continue with the subject of choice? In energy we experience all and are aware of a myriad of knowledge beyond the scope of humans at this point. So the life paths chosen are created in an environment that includes all of that knowledge. We try to remember what being "in body" is like when making those soul choices, but often we believe our souls can accomplish so much in one lifetime that the path we set is nearly impossible for the human self. That is the most concerning part of this process of laying out a life path. We are constantly hearing your human-self rail against the FATES over what is happening to you. And because of the pain you experience in human form we suffer with you. Knowing we were there when you chose these experiences, knowing you wanted the challenge to your soul self, but also knowing the pain that is overwhelming you is suffocating any connection you have to your soul self. We do not watch from here feeling superior to your human self. We watch and our heart energy experiences the pain with you. In a sense we are the tears you cry at your most desolate point. Our energy holds you in its arms and tries to comfort even though the pain you feel blocks the ability to feel us. Our energetic hearts flow along your life path with you because we are committed to your souls' journey. Each of you has this commitment from a group combining their energy for you. We do this for each other, because the process of learning, experiencing and evolving brings us back HOME; to our source, to our oasis, to our oneness with all that is. But this journey home is not a race; it is not to be won by one soul besting another. It is a pilgrimage in which all souls take a part and all will reach the destination together.

ENERGY

Here I am at our open door awaiting
your words to fill this space . . .

Like the winds you hear blowing outside your home, energy
blows through each of you and through each day, directed by
your thoughts and your focus. This energy is the life-giving
essence; it is the initial source of existence. It is God's breath.
What you focus on and put your energy into you bring to
life. Dwelling on the positive, gives life to the positive in your
existence, dwelling on the negative, gives life to the negative
in your existence. It is very simple in theory, very difficult in
practice. Human minds have a habit of being untrained, like an
unruly pet that will not behave, and gets into all kinds of trouble.
When the mind is trained, like an obedient pet, it adds joy and
love and comfort to your life. That mind can be the vehicle that
takes you everywhere you want to go; with no drama and with
peace. The obedient mind is a God send. In it the use of energy
is like the spreading of wealth in the world. It passes through
you and becomes a gift to all you meet and to every situation
you encounter. Developing an obedient mind is not a difficult
thing, it just takes time and training, just like a small pet. You
can train your mind not to react, but instead, to act upon any
given situation. An obedient mind does not get caught up in
the energy of others, it listens and loves. It shares its clarity, not
with words but with energy poured from the valves of its heart.

COMPANIONS/PURPOSE (PERSONAL)

Here I am at our open door awaiting
your words to fill this space . . .

You chose two very strong energy sources to companion
with you in the latter part of this journey of yours. Frances
is the equivalent of a multiple and variable energy conduit.
Brenda's contribution is her power and unflinching focus
of who she is and what HOME is. You three have walked
many life paths together, always supportive of each other and
always, to varying degrees gaining knowledge, experience and
growth in ways not possible as the pure energy on this side.

The link among the three of you is not just that you love and
care about each other, it is the core essence that binds us all. In
the three of you that core essence has grown, sharpened and
melded together in a close uniformity. You can be separated for
long periods of time but that core energy will always provide
a comfortable zone to gather yourselves together again. This
happens with souls that have direction and purpose to their
reentry into physical life time after time. There are souls who
chose easy and fun over driven and purposeful. You can see
that in all societies around your globe. But the three of you
have always chosen purpose. And have most often chosen
to support each other in that purpose. This life has been
particularly challenging for Brenda and Frances. Watching
from here has brought pain to our energetic hearts. As we said
before we are the tears you weep when you are at your most
desolate. The energy for those tears is ours, because we know
in crying them some of the pain will be released and it is easier

for you to connect with the essence of who you are. Pain, anger, rage, desolation and fear separate you from who you are, and form a boundary of emotion that keeps you from being able to connect with this side. Try to remember when you are in pain or fear that we are near even though you cannot feel us.

Each of you has "side angels" who also join in these journeys. You can identify them by their steadiness in your life, they come to teach or support, or share burdens. They comfort and uplift but may remain on your path for comparatively short distances.

Health/Fitness (Personal)

Here I am at our open door awaiting
your words to fill this space . . .

We must address an issue that is close to your concern. You are
not taking care of your physical body as would be best for it.
The lack of physical exercise, and the over indulgence in food
is causing lethargy and fatigue. You no longer need this extra
weight. You used it as an anchor to keep you in your body and
for other reasons because of your relationships. But you have
trained your mind and it is obedient to your needs now, so you
are capable and able to shrink your physical self into a healthy
and vibrant physical state. You will do this by a commitment to
exercise and to eating good healthy food in proper quantities.
You have the strength of mind and purpose to begin this leg of
your journey. So, for your physical self, please do so. We want to
see you healthy and vibrantly alive in this life and during this
creative adventure we have undertaken; being good to yourself
means treating yourself as a loved one, with kindness and
care. It means making thoughtful choices and enjoying each
choice because it aids you in becoming the out-picturing of who
you really are. It's ok for your soul self to shine without being
covered over with dimming weight. This is not a criticism of
what your physical body has become only truthful information
that the time has come for a dismantling of old ideas and the
behaviors that perpetuate them. We will help you with this
new mindset. Our purpose and our cause is that you be all
that you entered this life journey to express and become.

ERIC (PERSONAL)

Here I am at our open door awaiting
your words to fill this space . . .

We were sorry that you were upset by the news of your coworker
Eric. He is teetering on the threshold. He is about to come
Home. Eric's life was not a failure. He came to experience
what it was like to have and to lose a family. He made choices
that gave him great pain, and his soul made it through those
experiences, and will have learned a great deal from them,
as will all the souls that chose to be a part of his life. Here all
experience is of benefit, nothing is looked upon as a waste.
Your prayers for him are heard and his soul is rewarded by
them. It isn't possible to explain the rejoicing here when a
soul returns. It somehow completes us all more fully. Rejoice
in the time Eric was in your life, rejoice in the laughter and
the closeness shared by his friends and family. Those are the
legacies he leaves behind. Remember him for those, and not
for what your world perceives as bad choices and bad behavior.
All choices have purpose. All souls contribute something of
their essence to each one they touch. So remember how he
touched your life with laughter and love. Bless his soul for his
contribution to your life experience, and say a thankful prayer
for him. We will embrace his spirit upon its return to us.

Going Home

Here I am at our open door awaiting
your words to fill this space . . .

This idea of moving from your world to ours is filled with
pain on your side and received with rejoicing on our side.
It is seen as an ending for you but a return to the norm for
us. Like a child returning from college or a friend returning
from an extended trip. There are stories and experiences to
be shared, wonderful feelings to explore and an abundance
of growth to be assessed. Each soul's life experience adds to
the whole and enriches us all. They are oceans of love and
awareness that keep surging toward the goal of wholeness and
oneness with everything. We relish the chances for growth
and learning that are undertaken with each new life.

DAYS AND CONNECTIONS

Here I am at our open door awaiting
your words to fill this space . . .

Each of your days is a journey and an opportunity to become
more of who you desired to be when you started this life path.
No day goes unnoticed. No day is without its opportunities for
grace and growth. Days are not just days piled upon days without
awareness or adventure, unless you choose to see them as such.
Each one is a special page in your book of this lifetime. Each
one is filled with your consciousness about the world around
you. The people you interact with are all souls like yourself who
chose to walk a life path and chose to meet you there. There
are always reasons for connections. Meet each of these souls
with an enthusiasm for finding the reason for the connection
and you will flourish in this life you have planned. At the
super conscious level we know each other and our stories, we
all know the reasons we seek each other out; but bringing that
knowledge to our conscious minds while in human form takes
focus, dedication to the task and an obedient mind; a mind that
won't get caught up in the drama and will look into the heart
and see with your souls eyes the beauty that is there, the purpose
behind the script in your particular play. So walking thru your
life aware and willing to see and experience what you came
for is essential to your successful completion of this life path.

THE CHAOS OF LIFE

Here I am at our open door awaiting
your words to fill this space . . .

On a day filled with activity and chores we note that it is difficult
for you to calm your mind and be a clear conduit. We are
constantly amazed at the juggling that everyone does in your
physical world. It seems as the years go by that more and more
must be stuffed into all of the minutes of your days. There is
little or no time for simple quiet, or for introspection. No time
to discover who you are with television, magazines, newspapers,
computers, cell phones, blackberrys, ipods, ipads, and radios
jamming the space in your head with a chaotic swarm of
messages about the needs, wants and must haves; the wars, death
and struggle, hate, threat and worry, discord and discourse on
everything from A to Z. Where is the time to know who you are?
Where is the time to discover your purpose and path? Where is
the time to think positive, creative, life affirming thoughts? That
will only happen when each of you as individuals stop and make
the time. Bow out of the rat race and reach for something higher
and better. There are those around your globe who do this now.
They are the stabilizing forces. Their numbers are growing, and
they will continue to grow. Because sooner or later everyone in
body must stop and say "Why am I here?" Sooner or later the TV
will be turned off and the 24 hour news cycle will be ignored
and people will think for themselves; when that happens, the
world will awaken to its potential, to its possibilities, and to its
opportunities to create. These daily sessions are just a small step
in getting there. But as we each do our part, as a whole we will
all take one step closer to the day when we reclaim ourselves
and take our first conscious breath as a spirit in a human body.

Opportunities and Ego (Personal)

Here I am at our open door awaiting
your words to fill this space . . .

You have lately been exploring some routes to understanding
who you are and where your path now lies, routes that you
have not explored previously in this existence. We applaud
this curiosity. We also know that you planned well for your
meetings on your life path with those who were qualified to
give you information and encouragement that will push you
further down this path you have chosen. Each soul has these
guideposts implanted in their lives so that along the way they
have chance after chance to follow the path they were meant
to take. Being consciously aware of what is going on around
you, and taking the opportunities presented to you, even when
you may think you are not interested or ready, is one of the
ways you move toward your purpose. With all the mind clutter
infecting your lives it is very difficult to identify and soak up
the information at the guideposts, but the information is
always there. Open your eyes and take a look around. There
are opportunities everywhere. The special ones, made just for
you, the ones with your name on them, will come to you in
the most serendipitous ways. Through a series of friends or
acquaintances, through an overheard conversation, or a word in
an ad that catches your eye. But always with these particularly
important invitations you will know by a strong feeling inside.
That feeling can either be one of excitement about the
possibility, or, if the ego is involved, it can be one of fear, doubt,
or absolute rejection of the idea. That is how ego works, to
keep you on the safe and mundane path, the path which does

not threaten its possession of you. It will fill the opportunities presented with overtones of dislike or fear, doubt or aversion. The ego's job is to keep you physically safe and functioning at the highest level possible for a human in your situation. But some of you let the ego take too much control. It becomes the owner and director, the principal player in all your choices and scenarios. That is not to your benefit. The ego must be tamed just as the mind must be tamed. It must be trained to act and behave for the benefit of the soul's purpose here. When that is the case all opportunities presented are embraced and the information made available is absorbed, adding to the wealth of knowledge and direction the soul needs to achieve its purpose.

PICTURES OF REALITY

Here I am at our open door awaiting
your words to full this space . . .

The phone conversation that kept you from our morning
appointment was pertinent to what we will cover today. You
have often said, and repeated it again this morning, "that
each person sees events through their own picture of reality".
That statement is more than just true, it is the crux of all the
misunderstandings, judgments, anger, fear, and discord in
your physical world. There will never be a time when every
human being sees the world or circumstances in exactly the
same way. Therefore understanding that statement is what
needs to happen . . . on a world wide scale! Listening to
someone and understanding that the words and emotions
are coming from the sum total of their experiences, which
can never be the same as the sum total of your experiences,
is where true communication begins. It is in that place
of understanding that you need to honor their viewpoint
simply because it is uniquely <u>their</u> viewpoint. No one else is
standing in their shoes, only them . . . so their viewpoint is
valid, even though you may not agree with it, because it is
what they see from their unique perspective. Understanding
this and honoring their statements and feelings has the effect
of softening your response. There is no need to be right all
the time. There is a need to honor and understand that each
person's vision will be as different as each person's life path,
because no two souls ever choose exactly the same life path.

Schedules/Love (Personal)

Here I am at our open door awaiting
your words to fill this space . . .

As you can see from your own life, which has slowed tremendously
over the last 2 and a half years, there are still many occasions when
your commitment to something higher than yourself is put on hold
in order to accommodate life as you know it in human form. This is
not a criticism. It is merely a statement of fact as we see it. There is
no need to apologize each time you do not make it to our appointed
time. We know what is occurring, and will be available when time
permits you to be here with us. We realize that this commitment
is becoming easier and more enjoyable, if we can use that word,
for you. There is far less stressful energy around you when you
sit and transcribe information now. This makes the process
easier for all, and encourages us that you feel safe in this space.

We would like to address the subject of love, since a celebration
of that concept has just passed. What you know of as this
feeling falls very short of what we interpret your word to mean.
We find it difficult to identify with an emotion that promotes
intimacy as well as jealousy, honoring and anger, giving and
possessiveness, selflessness and abuse. We understand that all
of these emotions, which wrap themselves around this word
Love, are choices. But do you realize that they are choices.
Many of them seem to pop fully formed into your collective
minds and are acted upon without a modicum of actual
thought being given. This is where most paths go awry. This
is also where most lessons can be learned, and where grace
can be developed and exalted; because grace in love is the
highest form of love. It is the love that reaches beyond your
understanding and breathes the freshness of God into your lives.

14

LOVE

Here I am at our open door awaiting
your words to fill this space . . .

The outpouring of experiences and feelings you received in
your e-mail today regarding your friend Eric touches upon
the true concept of love that we experience here. The people
who touched Eric's life and whose life he touched shared
more than just time and workplace functions, more than just
common interests and friendship. This honoring of another
soul and that souls' journey through life is a special level
of soul commitment one soul can give another as you walk
along your life path. It is the understanding that each soul
will choose its direction and that those around him may
not agree with the choice, but will respect the soul's right to
make it. This outpouring of understanding and acceptance
is truly an expression of love at its most pure, untainted by
any judgment or anger. It is a releasing of the loved soul
with prayers in their hearts for a happy reunion at Home.
Nothing could be a better measure of a souls' worth.

MARY ANN (PERSONAL)

Here I am at our open door awaiting
your words to fill this space . . .

As you experienced today, with the reading of the astrological
chart for your sister, there are many clues to the life path
chosen by any soul. Keeping your heart and mind open to
the ideas and inspirations that come to you is the best way
to link into any of those clues. Seeking to understand the
clues by relating them to your life experience is the fastest
way to walk your dedicated path. Seekers are always rewarded
with information. That information can highlight what has
caused divergences from the life path or can give momentum
to speed you more easily and quickly in the direction you
were meant to take. Mary Ann released some highly stressful
energy today and was physically able to note the difference. It
must be said here that the little girl who danced in the living
room to the delight of all who saw her is still there with her
and is struggling to be acknowledged and let free to dance
again. The spirit of her mother would like nothing better
than to see that happen! From your mother's soul this must
be said. Mary Ann has followed her life path faithfully to this
point. She made no mistakes, no errors in judgment. The
souls she met and married agreed to dance this life dance
with her for part of her life path. All parties agreed to this
interchange of time to create an avenue to glean what they
needed from each other. Some of the learning caused her
pain, but she has risen above that pain and extracted the
positive sense of self from each encounter that allowed her to
walk away from relationships that could not honor her soul
self. This is a wonderful achievement, a growth of soul spirit
that is hard won in the physical world, but is impossible to

win in our energetic existence. Soul growth is why we choose to lay out life paths and enter the physical world. It is the only way our souls advance in achieving all the expanded understanding we need in order to return to our source.

OBEDIENT MIND

Here I am at our open door awaiting
your words to fill this space . . .

We wish to return to the "Obedient Mind" idea. We know that
this notion does not resonate with most people. You think
of your mind as a busy hive of mental activity if you think of
it at all. But your mind is a tool just as your body is a tool. It
is one of the most important tools if not <u>the most important</u>
tool. Harnessing and directing the activity of the mind with
purpose and determination gives you a mind/body link that
strengthens both the mind and the body exponentially. What
goes on outside your body you do not have any control over.
But what goes on inside your body you have complete control
over if you choose to accept it. This can only be achieved by
practice and the best form of practice is meditation. You can do
active or passive meditation, whichever suits your temperament
and personality. But we strongly suggest that meditation
should be a daily practice in each life. The reasons for this
are many. It is a perfect way to touch the core of your being, it
calms and centers the mind and filters out all the extraneous
chatter and energy that surrounds you, it has the effect of
not only quieting the mind but enhancing the health of the
body, it allows you to create a free flow of energy throughout
your body, ridding it of all the blocks caused by stress, worry,
negativity and fear. In essence meditation is a one size fits all
cure for many of the most common ills of the physical body.
If being still is a problem for you, you can still meditate by
sitting in a rocking chair and just rocking. But while rocking
keep your mind focused on one calming thought or image.
Don't be stressed if your mind wanders, just gently bring it
back to the calming thought or image. Eventually your mind

will stay focused and that allows healing work to be done in the body. Clearing the mind of the clutter of chaotic thoughts is like cleaning your home, or organizing your desk, it gives you the opportunity to claim this space as your own and to use it to your advantage. This is the most powerful tool you were given as a soul in a human body, but the majority of people have no idea of the chaos they allow to reign in their minds.

MISUSE OF ENERGY

Here I am at our open door awaiting
your words to fill this space . . .

Energy is a quantitative force. It also is a tool, one that can be used
in many different ways for many different purposes. The most
effective and most ethical use for energy is to protect and heal.
There are a host of groups that can teach the effective use of energy.
There are also many people who use energy to harm others. Like
any tool it can be misused just as the mind can be misused. But the
misuse of energy can cause harm to others. This is a concept that
has eluded humankind. You misuse energy every day. Anger, fear,
rage, maliciousness, jealousy, envy; all the negative emotions are a
misuse of energy. Like inserting a battery to empower an electronic
instrument, your battery is your life energy. You misuse that
energy every time you focus your anger or any negative emotion
on anyone or anything. That energy empowers your words and
actions, and is directed outward toward the object of your negative
emotion. Any living thing in the path of that energy is affected
by its contaminating negativity. This happens billions of times
every day in your world, and humankind is totally oblivious to it.

We note, Sharon that you have a habit of cleansing your energy
each night before retiring and we are in total agreement
that such should be the case for everyone. That cleansing
eliminates any negative contaminants and gives you a clean
energy field in which to rest and restore your body. There are
many very simple ways to do this cleansing and you are aware
of most of them. Spread that information to all you know; do
not be concerned about whether they understand or believe
you, or whether they follow your advice. That choice is for
them to make, all you need to do is share the information.

20

VIEWPOINTS

Here I am at our open door awaiting
your words to fill this space . . .

"Agreeing to disagree" is one of your favorite statements.
Embodied in that statement is the seed of all understanding
about how your world could work so much more efficiently
and peacefully. Agreeing to disagree implicitly understands
that there is more than one viewpoint in any debate. It also
recognizes the need to honor all viewpoints. Note, we did not say
agree with all viewpoints only to understand that each viewpoint
is filtered through that persons picture of reality. That picture is
exclusively the property of that person. No one else has walked
in their shoes or seen their life experience through their eyes.
So understanding that they have arrived at their viewpoint the
same way you have arrived at yours is essential in understanding
that both are valid. You may not agree, but honoring the process
that creates the viewpoint is mandatory if peace is ever to reign
on earth. Teaching this simple tenet would go a long way in
creating generations of children with a core understanding
that disagreement on certain issues does not create enemies.
On the contrary it opens doors that, if explored, give new
understanding and insight into life itself. Understanding that
can bring the honoring of each individual to a much higher level
than ever before. Knowledge about what has shaped and colored
another person's thought process can only enhance your own.

PATHWAYS

Here I am at our open door awaiting
your words to fill this space . . .

This year will be one of great change for many people in
your world. As you have often said 11 is an important number
and provides an open door to many possibilities. There are
opportunities pending for most of the people you know
personally, opportunities that will take them in new directions if
they are willing to walk through that open door. Holding tightly
to what they have in their lives now will hinder their progress
and delay the journey along their life path. Don't misunderstand,
that doesn't mean that these opportunities will never come
again. They will come again, but the time wasted by deferring
the choice to walk through the door can never be retrieved.
Pathways unexplored are one of the sharpest regrets returning
souls bring Home with them. Pathways that are rejected until
later in life are also regretted simply because so much more
could have been accomplished if the soul had chosen that path
when the door first opened to them. We tell you these things
not to push you into areas you don't feel ready for, and not to
make you feel less than the truly wonderful souls you are. We tell
you just so you have the necessary information from this side to
weigh in the balance with all your other information when an
opportunity presents itself. When that happens, when you are
faced with the choice of a new path as an option in your life,
consider all you normally would consider, but also go inside.
Stop the chaos in your heart and in your mind, and listen to
your Higher Self and take heed of what you find there. Add
that to the sum total of your earthly concerns so that you have a
balanced scale of information from which to make your choice.
Then move forward with no regrets, whichever path you choose.

Choosing—Getting Involved or Not

Here I am at our open door awaiting
your words to fill this space . . .

You had a very clear example of viewpoints and "pictures
of reality" today. It would have been very easy to become
wrapped up in the drama of the energetic exchange you
witnessed. We are very glad you chose not to engage in that
fruitless exercise. As we said before, this happens billions
of times every day in your world. There are many lessons
being learned through the process. And those lessons are
there to be learned by all who choose to become enrapt
in the drama of whatever energy is being exchanged.
Consciously choosing to stand back and allow those who
wish to participate to grab the drama and make it their
own, simply means that this is one lesson you have already
learned. Bless those who are participating in it and allow
them the freedom to do so. It is their choice and is for their
eventual growth that they do. If you must add your energy
in some way to what is occurring, then pray that they will
learn their lessons quickly and resolve their issues peacefully
and harmoniously; more than that you cannot do. This
seems to be one of the most difficult decisions for a soul
in the body to make. Standing back and allowing the play
of energy being exchanged between two or more people to
run its course without being drawn into the fray is just very
difficult in most instances. Whether because you feel a need
to protect one of the parties, or because something inside
you that is in your picture of reality is pressing to be said or
expressed in some way. Taking hold of your mind and pushing

it to look clearly at the flow of feelings and energy being displayed is allowing your higher self to add its information to the experience, and with that higher-self information you can usually bring calm to chaos and peace to conflict.

2012

Here I am at our open door awaiting
your words to fill this space . . .

We wish to speak of coming changes today, but your mind is
unwilling to remain clear enough for us to do this. We require
a clear path to send the information we have, and this subject
is causing you to tense up. Though that may be an involuntary
action it still hinders the pathway. Let us try this again.

The next almost 2 years will see an increase in the information
regarding the realignment of planets. As your scientists and
astrologers have realized this realignment has not happened
for more than 26,000 years, so no one has any information to
look back on to give you a clue what will take place. Without
the knowledge of historical specifics to refer to speculation will
abound. What we wish you to know is that each soul walking
the earth right now chose to be there at this specific time.
So each of you has something to contribute, something you
bring to the planet's energy that you wanted to provide at this
specific time. The more that the idea grows that you are all in
this journey together the sooner you will be able to avoid the
talk of cataclysmic events that cloud your thinking. The idea
that the magnetic pull of these planets as they align could
cause massive destruction on earth is just an IDEA. Ideas don't
have any power until you put your belief in them; that is when
your focus and your energy become involved, and you start to
create your own outcome. So our suggestion is that your time
and energy would be much more wisely used by focusing on
now, and on understanding that you are all on that beautiful
planet at this perfect time in order to create whatever you
will. The choice of that creation is your own. Choose wisely.

FRUSTRATIONS OF LIFE

Here I am at our open door awaiting
your words to fill this space . . .

Your conversation with Brenda this morning brings up more information about choices. Planning a life path and knowing all the opportunities you will be given while walking that path is one thing. Living a life in your physical world, fraught with all the indecision, questions, choices, expectations and obstacles is entirely another. For a highly spiritual soul in a human body, who chose a life almost entirely of service to others, it is agonizing. When a physical being who knows enough about her higher self to be aware, while she is in physical form, of the vast differences and limitless possibilities of our world, the inability to manifest what she knows becomes overwhelming.

This has been Brenda's situation for many years. Her life path tied her to a contract of service to others, which she has completed with the vigor of one who is fully aware of the soul self in each human form. She has loved and honored each one as they have appeared on her life path. That loving and honoring is the core of her spirit, it is what makes her unique among souls. She enriches every life she touches. But then she looks at her own life through the lens of a human being and says," I am more than this, why can't I manifest who I am?!" This cry from the soul we hear loudly and clearly. This is one of the most difficult things about being spiritually aware. That sense of knowing is so much a part of you that you actually ache to feel and experience and live in that truth and energy. As wonderful as that knowing can be it can also be a double edged sword. If your life path, chosen by you, does not give you an opening to express more of who you are, you feel stuck in a life that in no way out pictures what you know to be true about yourself. In this case the sense of futility and fruitlessness can be all consuming, as though there is no purpose at all to being. We have watched this time and time again with very strong souls who, in spirit, feel that they will be able to cope with the challenges they place on their life path. The physical reality however is often far more difficult to handle than can be realized in spirit. We are not walking the physical path you chose so there is very little we can do to take away the pain you feel because of the difference between what you know and what you see before you. Your soul self was the architect of your life path and that soul self must be the touchstone you go to when you feel overwhelmed with what your physical life is showing you. That soul self is the only place you will be able to find the shift in perspective that is needed to focus on walking the path chosen and accomplishing the tasks undertaken in this life.

QUIETING THE MIND

Here I am at our open door awaiting
your words to fill this space . . .

We would like to return to an idea that seems to have little or no relevance in your world. That is the idea of quieting the mind and the pace of your lives, at least for a few minutes every day. The thought that quiet time is wasted seems to permeate your global society. This could not be further from the truth. Getting caught up in the need for multitasking is driving humans to focus outwardly in their search for happiness, satisfaction and peace. None of those cherish goals will be found outside yourselves. These are destinations only found within. This concept is one that is eluding humankind to a great extent. If you allow for a quiet space, just a short time each day, perhaps fifteen or twenty minutes, to shut out and shut off every instrument of distraction, you will find an inner ability to recharge your personal batteries, to reconnect with who you really are, to listen to your soul self and reacquaint yourself with the purpose and promise of this life you have chosen. The rewards for becoming quiet each day are many, but probably the most interesting one would be realizing how addicted you have become to the noise and distraction. Why does most of your global society need to be contacted, connected or entertained nearly 18 hours out of every day? What is it you are trying so hard to avoid or shut out? The technology in your world is amazing and wonderful. It allows communication on a level never seen before, a level never imagined. But the down side is that human to human communication and individual time to decompress is minimal, thus the chance to realize the value of each human and the time to really know your own value is lost in an echo chamber of voices, noises, demands and timelines that have everything to do with functioning in the physical world, and absolutely nothing to do with the reason you are there or the life you came to live. Do yourselves the incredible favor of coming to know the true you by setting aside time to be still and visit your soul self, to become acquainted with the part of you that is eternal, the part of you that is the Breath of God.

COMMUNICATION

Here I am at our open door awaiting
your words to fill this space . . .

We wish to discuss "communicating with love". Much of what
passes for communication in your human world is simply a
series of monologues between two or more people. One speaks
then the other speaks, but in between speaking, there is no
listening. When one is not speaking they are figuring out
what to say next, thus there is no real communication there
are only 2 separate monologues. This is so prevalent in your
world no one really notices any more, but the result of these
isolated and isolating conversations is that the distance between
people is growing so quickly it is extremely rare to see an actual
conversation where the art of listening is the main component.
Listening is something that is not taught any longer. People
speak at or to one another but rarely with each other. Without
true involved, earnest and heartfelt communication there will
never be a space for true peace on your planet. When we speak
of true conversation we are not just talking about the lack of
listening skills, but the lack of engaging any of your senses in
having a conversation. This means watching the body language
of the person you are speaking with, making eye contact with
them and sensing from your soul what their energy is telling
you about them. Communication is a total body/mind/spirit
function. If that is not what you do in your day to day living then
you are missing one of the most valuable resources you have
as human beings. Bringing all of your senses to the table in a
conversation not only honors who you are in all your aspects,
but it also honors the person and the soul with whom you are
conversing. In conversations such as these differences become
meaningless, the understanding and honoring of each other

is the goal and the outcome. Yes, this is a very different way to look at having a conversation, but a conversation is a gift of your time and attention, treat it like a gift. Take the time to invest it with all of your interest and intellect, all of your energy and discernment. Listen with your heart and see, with the eyes God gave you, the soul within the other person. Don't miss these opportunities to spread the gifts of your soul to those you come in contact with each day. Soon you will find that having a conversation the old way is like looking at your old silent movies when compared to your new 3D movies. Silent movies were wonderful in their time, but technology has evolved and so must mankind in the way you communicate.

USING ENERGY EFFECTIVELY

Here I am at our open door awaiting
your words to fill this space . . .

Now we wish to discuss the simple things that can uplift a
person and change their energy. There are several ways to
modify the energy we all work in. We say "work in" on purpose
because that is exactly what we do and what you do. Although
mankind has yet to understand this concept fully, it is, none
the less, an accurate statement and exactly the right phrase to
use. Humans are surrounded by an energy field; your scientists
have proved this. You use that energy every day in everything
you do. Coming in contact with others can be an uplifting
and energy heightening experience, or a depleting and energy
draining experience. Sometimes you allow others to pollute
your energy field, which is very much like allowing someone to
dump their garbage in your living room. Most of you have no
idea this is happening but suddenly you feel angry, tired or upset
and cannot find a real reason for it. That is because you have
allowed someone to "dump on you". When you find yourself in
this situation and can find no real reason to be feeling poorly,
our suggestion is to find a quiet place for just a few minutes.
While in this quiet place we want you to imagine you are in a
bathroom. As you imagine yourself in the bathroom, we want
you to put your imaginary hand on the handle of the toilet
and flush it. Everyone is familiar with the sound of a flushing
toilet, as you hear the imaginary sound in your head visualize
a large vacuum hose in the center of the earth under your feet.
As the sound grows see the negative energy as a grey or black
dust cloud being pulled from your body leaving your energy
field and dropping down into the center of the earth. You
should immediately feel lighter and better. Laughter is another

way to clear and lighten your energy field. It works wonders. These are simple yet very effective practices that will serve you well if you use them regularly. Please remember that keeping your energy field clean keeps others from infecting you with their pollution, if you are clear and clean then so is your mind, and your heart can be fully in touch with your soul self.

PRAYER

Here I am at our open door awaiting
your words to fill this space . . .

The "power of prayer" is a precious resource. We have spoken
several times of the energy that surrounds each person, and have
said that your focus and intent is the driving force of that energy.
When you pray, regardless of the form of prayer you use, you are
focusing that energy with the specific words of your prayer. This
is why when many people pray with the same words and intent,
results are often noticeable. It is not because there is some super
being out in the universe that hears your prayers and acts on your
behalf. It is because you were given all the tools you need to bring
about the outcome you want. You just need the knowledge, focus
and dedication to use them appropriately. Sharon, you pray every
day, a prayer that you have designed for yourself, a prayer which
covers all the areas you want your focus drawn toward. We also note
that most of your prayer is a prayer of gratitude. Energy focused on
gratitude for the world around you builds a bond with that world.
It creates a symbiotic relationship with that world. Gratitude is one
of the most powerful emotions on which to dwell. It enhances the
consciousness of all the people in the world who wish to focus on
what can aid, heal, help, and prevent the pockets of negativity you
now see. Don't ever give up on prayer. It is one of the strongest tools
you have. It creates great strength in your energy field. It brightens
and invigorates the energy field. This is one of the reasons you
feel so much peace after your prayers. There are prayerful people
all over your globe, people who are balancing the energy of your
planet daily by their dedication to prayer. This is something
that will be needed more and more often over the coming
years. Prayer raises the collective consciousness, allows room for
positive growth and enhances lives with a clearer perspective.

LETTING GO (PERSONAL)

Here I am at our open door awaiting
your words to fill this space . . .

You are currently torn between two situations you feel the need to handle. You are allowing yourself to become embroiled in trying to make everything fit right and get it all planned out. Stop. Stop figuring and planning and trying to make something that involves other people happen the way you feel it should. All you need to do is offer your assistance and availability to the universal energy and "see" the outcome you are praying for happen. That is all. Focus your energy on the happy outcome and let the focus of your energy work out the rest of the details. You are making it too complicated and too emotional. Let go of the need to handle it all. Allow us to intercede on your behalf and all will work out the way it should for all the parties involved. We know that you have been grappling with this situation for many months, but putting negative worry and angst into it is fruitless and it hinders the process. Use the energy tools we have revealed in the manner they are meant to be used, and then let go. That is probably the most difficult part for humans, letting go. Your world applauds a hands-on attitude. So you are used to being involved in every little aspect of any project. But that is not how this energy concept works. All you need to do is formulate the idea of a willingness to go, be or do something, and focus only on the end result. Then you must let it go. The letting go and trusting that the energy you expended in creating the idea and the willingness to create the outcome by doing all you can personally, are enough to propel the idea to its completion. Trust that the God part of you will take over and all will be well.

RELATIONSHIPS

Here I am at our open door awaiting
your words to fill this space . . .

Today we will speak of relationships. You have already been
told that life paths are set out by each soul. The relationships
programmed for a life are established before that human life
begins. All energies involved in the main focuses of that life
are in agreement to interact at various points along the life
path. Intimate and very close relationships are one of the most
important ways to experience that which cannot be experienced
here in energy form. Here there is all knowledge and knowing,
a total understanding of each energy form. In human form that
information is wiped away and each soul in human form must
relearn how to connect. Most of you do that on a very surface
level, one that only touches the physical and sometimes the
mental levels. But to have a relationship which encompasses all
levels, mental, emotional, physical and spiritual, is to have the
gift of total immersion in another persons' soul. This is what
each relationship is meant to be striving for, because in that
deep sharing of who you really are you experience the honesty
of soul to soul communication. There are many intersecting
ideas, motivations, people, dramas, and focuses that encompass
a life in your world, and each of these can become a stumbling
block to a true relationship. Too many times you are unwilling
to give the attention to your loved one that is needed to create
a safe space in which to truly experience each other. You will
keep trying for that relationship which feeds your soul but you
will not get there without the clear sightedness that knowing
yourself as a soul being can give you. If you are unwilling to
know your true self you will never be able to truly know another.

BEING PRESENT

Here I am at our open door awaiting
your words to fill this space . . .

We are with you today to speak of stopping chaotic thought
processes. It is difficult for you to comprehend how much
the constant mind chatter does to impede your knowledge of
yourself. It is like trying to find that one pure station on a radio
with a million static signals coming through. You take no control
of your mind 80 percent of the time or more. You just allow
thoughts to rumble on through without any effort to monitor,
control or audit them. Most of these thoughts are errant mind
wanderings, or old tapes from your past, or running scenarios
of what might happen in the future. When you stop to really
think, and we invite you to do that far more often than you do
now, the only time you have to accomplish anything is right
now . . . which means that you are literally wasting the current
time you have with mindless chatter. We will remind you again
that learning to gain some measure of control over where your
mind goes and what it spends its time on can only work to
benefit your life in very significant ways. Learning to do this
is fairly easy, it is fairly painless and it is imperative. Now more
than ever it is necessary not to dwell on the past and the future,
but to live each of your days being fully present. As we have said
before, meditation is an excellent way to teach yourself how
to harness the power of your mind in realistic and productive
ways. There are many different techniques, we have mentioned
some very simple ones before, but whichever discipline for
meditation you use we ask that you use it on a daily basis. This
is the only way to harness the power of your mind and in the
process of doing so find and touch the truth of who you are.
Right now in your world these two things are imperative.

TALISMANS

Here I am at our open door awaiting
your words to fill this space . . .

We shall speak of talismans today. Humans often retain a
keepsake of a loved one after they depart. There are many and
varied reasons for this. Feeling a need for a connection to the
person who has passed is one of the most common reasons.
What we want to acknowledge is that the keepsake or talisman
is indeed a connection to that soul. First because the energy
of the departed soul has permeated the keepsake, and second
because the focusing on the talisman by the human holding
it brings the energy of the departed back in touch with the
human. There are abundant stories of this kind of energy
connection, and the strength of the bond it creates. The use
of talismans has come down through the ages, from the oldest
times to the present. They can give great comfort, and be a
great blessing when used properly. However, using a talisman for
more than just a touchstone would create a dependence on it.
That would mean that it becomes more of a focus than the life
you are committed to living. This is something to be avoided.
We do understand the deep loss and sense of emptiness when
a loved one is removed from your plane. However, grief is to be
experienced and worked through. A talisman would be a poor
substitute for the life you were meant to live. Keeping them as
touchstones honors the soul who has passed and the love that
was shared. Keeping it as more than that is detrimental to your
journey on your life path and should be avoided at all costs.

TIME

Here I am at our open door awaiting
your words to fill this space . . .

Time is something that causes concern to most humans. Either
there is not enough of it or it goes to fast, or you can't wait until
it passes so you can get to some experience you think you will
treasure. We understand that you live in a linear and time based
world, but when will you realize that the only time you have is
this moment? That the rest of your life grows from right now.
The rest of your life grows from right now! This is the moment
for choosing, doing, saying, being what is most important to you,
right now. So much of your time is used up in the onslaught of
timetables, chores, work, and all the parts and pieces that go
into a human life; that the most important thing of all gets lost
in the chaos. That is the fact that you are a soul in a human body
with a purpose for being . . . <u>a purpose for being!</u> Finding what
that purpose is opens the window of wonder and possibilities in
your life. It refreshes the air, and helps you to focus your efforts
on the goal you set for yourself. Whatever that goal is, attending
to it and reaching it is the reason for your existence in this place
and time. So how do you find out what your purpose is? First,
and we have said this before, quiet your mind, so that you can
touch the soul that you are. That means meditation of whichever
sort you choose. Second, there is that space, that area in each
of your lives that is rewarding for you; it just feels good and
right when you are in it, or doing it. That is the space or place,
the springboard from which you will find your purpose. Follow
that heartfelt drive and you will find your soul will be in all that
you do. Time will no longer be something that is past or future;
now will be where you live and breathe and have your life, this
life you planned. There is where you will find all your joy.

EXERCISE (PERSONAL)

Here I am at our open door awaiting
your words to fill this space . . .

We are aware of your difficulty in holding to your schedule
of exercise. We are also aware of the energizing benefits you
feel when you exercise consistently. We want you to know that
we are cheering for you in this change in your life patterns.
We do understand the difficulty in changing habits held for a
long period of time, we also understand that those habits are
tied to habits or patterns of thought that have also been held
for a long time. So we want to be very clear when we say that
you no longer need to carry the bulk of excess weight you are
carrying. It has served its purpose, and is no longer needed.
Please remember when you think about exercising that all of
the cells in your body are on your side. They all want to be
part of a healthy life form. So they are cheering for you too.
You will shed the extra weight, we know this to be true, for you
have committed to us to do this work and you will commit to
us and more importantly to yourself to eat healthy and exercise
for the strength and health of your body. Your mind is telling
you that this routine is a chore, and that is far from true, it is
the natural evolution of the body that is housing your soul.
That soul needs a strong and health home and you will provide
it. Remember this when you rise in the morning and it will
energize you to attend to your routine with joy in your heart.

LET GO OF FALSE CONTROL (PERSONAL)

*Here I am at our open door awaiting
your words to full this space . . .*

Our message is for you today. We have asked you to stop
worrying over the plans and responsibilities surrounding your
coming trip to your sister. You have expressed your wishes,
your intent, and your willingness to do whatever is necessary to
make it all proceed without incident or hardship for anyone.
It must be pointed out here that each person involved in this
plan has their own right to choose what they wish to have
happen on those days you will be gone. To the extent that our
energies can assist in the outcome you intend we will certainly
do so. Humans constantly forget that they can only order their
own choices and intentions. The rest of the souls involved
in the play get to write their own script. They get to choose
their own actions and their own intentions. Be true to what
you envision for this plan; then let it go. The world will not
fall apart because you are not here to help and be responsible
for the running of the home. Allow others the opportunity to
step up and take part. All will come about exactly as it should.
Quiet your mind of worry. It adds only negative energy and you
know better. Be still and allow what will be to be. Make your
plans and take control over your arrangements. There is no
need to hold off planning your timetable. Trust in the spirit
of those around you to fill in where and whenever necessary.

DREAMS

Here I am at our open door awaiting
your word to fill this space . . .

Dreams are the subject today. Most humans feel that dreams
are merely the product of an over stimulated brain; a brain
which, in sleep, dumps its overflow of chaotic images and
words. But that is very far from the truth. Dreams are
communication from your Higher Self, that part of you not
in body; the part of you which is closest to your Soul Self.
This aspect of yourself communicates through your dream
state when you are not taking the time to quiet your mind so
communication can happen in a meditative state. We strongly
suggest paying careful attention to your dreams, getting a
good dream book which is based on the spiritual aspects
of life, and looking up all the remembered parts of your
dreams to see what information you are being given. This
is a wonderful way to get clues about what is happening in
your life, what to be aware of, how to move forward. Keeping
a pen and small tablet by your bed is the best way to make
sure you remember your dreams. It is easy to forget them
when the rest of your life comes rushing in every morning.
Also the more unusual or terrifying a dream is the more
important it is . . . these are the dreams to really focus on,
because your higher self will use anything it knows will make
a strong impression on you to get you to remember a dream
when the message of the dream is exceptionally urgent.
Recurring dreams are also important, these dreams deal with
recurring issues in your life that your higher self is trying
to get you to recognize. They usually deal with situations or
stumbling blocks you keep setting up in your life. Looking at
the dream components and figuring them out is a great way

to get the insight needed to stop making the same mistake. Dreams are to be taken seriously. They are guide post along your life path. Dreams present you with ideas, knowledge and direction if you take the time to interpret them.

INTERPERSONAL RELATIONSHIPS

Here I am at our open door awaiting
your words to fill this space . . .

The most important area to focus on for a soul in a human body
is your interpersonal relationships. This is where most of the
growth you have planned can be experienced. The amount of
experience possible in one human life time is enormous. But
the growth of the soul within that lifetime is unimaginable if
attention is paid to the people coming in contact with you every
day. Whether on a long term basis or just a casual meeting, the
cashier at a checkout stand or the woman selling you movie
tickets; each of these souls crosses your life path to give you
a chance to be who you are in a fully present manner. This
chance, which comes to you a hundred times a day, is the chance
to express your souls' light without filter and without any effort
to mask it. This is not something humans do easily, it is a learned
behavior. It is a behavior that takes courage and belief and
the innate understanding that each of you is there for just this
purpose. To show your soul self to each other in a way that you
recognize in the deepest parts of yourselves. You may think that
this is an impossible goal, but it is a goal that each soul strives
to attain when planning a life path and initiating a life journey.
This isn't a choice taken lightly nor is it taken just as some lesson
to be ticked off of a list of chores to be done as a soul. It is the
reason we exist, it is the goal we all have; to become one with
that which created us. In order to do that we must be willing
to be the soul we are without reservation, without pretention,
and without fear. Doing this in human form is a formidable task
to say the least. The ego, which is a safety valve for the human

44

body, usually is given far too much control and makes this task
next to impossible because it deems the behavior too risky.
Strive to take your ego in hand and control its voice in your life.
The voice which must be the loudest is the voice of your soul,
always and in every situation. If that voice has your ear and your
heart the choices you make will be choices that will enhance
your life's journey and move you speedily along your life path.
Honor those souls you meet every day with your heightened
spiritual attention. What you see and learn will amaze you.
The insight you gather will fill your heart and illuminate
your soul. Don't deprive yourself of this experience because it
will feed your soul with the food of understanding and with
the vision that allows you to see the oneness in all things.

BODY, MIND, SPIRIT

Here I am at our open door awaiting
your words to fill this space . . .

You have a saying in your world: "What the mind can conceive, it can achieve." This concept gives you just some small idea of the power of the human mind. But that power grows to unlimited heights when coupled with your hearts intent and passion. Mind, heart and body are the foundation for the success of any endeavor; your mind for the concept, heart for the passion and drive, body for the energy or the physical carrying out of the plan. So many of you try to build your hopes and dreams on one or two of these and wonder why nothing concrete happens. A stool will not stand on one or even two legs; it needs the third for it to balance properly. Balance is what you need for any dream to come to fruition. Everything in your human world is about balance, about the need for all living things in your world to find a balance with each other and coexist in harmony. It is the same for your dreams and your goals; they take the harmony of body, mind and spirit (heart) in order to be realized. When the mind conceives a goal, it should send the idea to the heart for the heart to assess. This is where your soul self is able to take hold of the idea and imbue it with that sense of driving spirit, and then the body should be able to take over by taking whatever steps it can in the direction of the dream. We are not talking about big steps here we are talking about baby steps, while you allow the universe to set up and make ready the manifestation of the plan you have conceived, because that is how eternal energy or the universe works. When you link the three aspects needed to fulfill a dream and hold to that vision, you link into a universal drive that is answering your call. Like the Bat Signal you provide the Spotlight (your idea), the electrical outlet (your heart) and when they are connected, the beam into the night (your body's intention to follow through). All of these steps send your signal out to the universal energy asking for completion of this dream. As simple as this sounds coordinating the 3 and initiating the beam seems to be a difficult task for humans.

PLANET EARTH

Here I am at our open door awaiting
your words to fill this space . . .

You pray each day for those who are suffering in the midst of
natural and manmade disasters around your globe. Your prayers
are heard and added to the energy of all the others who pray for
those in areas of distress. This latest earthquake is an example
of what can happen when mans' greed outreaches his common
sense. Your earth is a treasure, it contains everything you need
to live fulfilling and well contented lives, but that does not seem
to be enough for some. There is a whole culture now in your
world that thrives on acquiring more, more of everything. So
the people, the plants and animals, and the environment are all
subject to this rampaging greed. The collective consciousness
of your planet must change if it is to survive. Each person,
one after the other, can change it. But the choice must be a
conscious mental choice from each of you. Doing what you can
from where you are to encourage others to open their eyes and
see, truthfully what is being done to your home. There is no
other place in the universe exactly like your Earth. With all of its
natural beauty, all of its rich resources, and all of the possibilities
it holds, you still don't understand what a treasure you have
been given. Perhaps with this current onslaught of disasters
natural and otherwise a light bulb will turn on and people will
begin to understand to some small extent the responsibility
that is theirs. This cannot be ignored for much longer. Many of
you are feeding the collective consciousness that will allow for
a rejuvenation of the earth, but many, many more are needed.
Right now there is might and energy moving toward using all
the resources available and "damn the consequences". But there
is a slow and steady group which is always moving forward to

enrich and enhance what has been misused or over used. This movement toward appreciation and regard for your global home is encouraging to see. Please propel it forward with all the focus and energy you can. The rewards will be unbelievable.

INVEST IN NOW

Here I am at our open door awaiting
your words to fill this space . . .

Time is our topic tonight since it is something you try to manipulate
with the changing of your clocks to make the daylight seem to
last longer. It is a way you see as a tool to preserve resources. But
this, like so many other things, is just a way to make yourselves feel
more in control of an environment over which you have no control.
Time moves on at the same pace it always does. Hours turn to
days, days to weeks, weeks to months, etc. Nothing you do changes
that. Rather than playing with your clocks you would be better
served by inhabiting the moments you have, moment by moment.
Be invested in them, pay attention to them. From here we see so
much passing you by unnoticed. Look around you and see with
all your being what is in your field of vision. But don't just see with
your eyes, you have other senses that can feed you information
about your surroundings. Your eyes give your mind a picture, your
mind analyzes that picture, what you see and analyze should impact
your emotions in some way, but you don't give what you see your
focus and attention, so you don't have time to feel with your heart.
You miss so much by hurrying through your day and spending
your time thinking about the next thing that needs to be done, or
tomorrow when there will be other things to do. Even though you
know those things will be there when it is time to do them, you
waste your NOW, focusing on the future or the past, or what might
have been, or hoping for what may yet happen. The treasure you
seek is in the present moment. This is all you have in your hands
right now, live it, and live in it. So many opportunities exist in the
NOW; opportunities to love, to express, to truly see someone, to
truly be there for someone. Don't waste the precious time you
have on earth by missing the moment in which you are living.

LIVING CONSCIOUSLY

Here I am at our open door awaiting
your words to fill this space . . .

Consciousness is the topic for tonight. Living consciously is
apparently difficult for humankind. It is so easy to be caught
up in your routines; to be caught up in the trivialities of daily
living that the big picture is lost. Sometimes the big picture is
never even considered. The big picture we are speaking of is
your reason for being in body in the first place. You entered this
life because you had a purpose in mind; because you wanted
to contribute something, or experience something, or achieve
something. But there was a purpose. In the course of a human
life that purpose sometimes becomes lost or buried under the
cares and worries of everyday life. Our request is that you start
looking for that purpose. You will know it when you find it. It
will resonate within your heart. It will be something that speaks
to you in a way you cannot ignore. Finding this purpose for
yourself is probably the best thing you can do for yourself right
now. This purpose doesn't have to be something great. Your
world is so centered on the larger than life accomplishments
of a few people, that ordinary, everyday humans feel there is
little they could contribute. This could not be further from
the truth. You touch lives every day. When you identify your
purpose you will be able to touch those lives with this newly
imbued sense of spiritual purpose, and the difference that
will make will astound you. You will see your world through
different eyes, through eyes that are focused on the soul self
in each person you meet. Seeing that soul self, and honoring
it makes each person you come in contact with a spiritual
treasure to be enjoyed and acknowledged. We watch you pass
each other each day of your lives never looking closely enough

to see who you really are, how you really shine, or how each particular soul fits into the puzzle of this life you have chosen. Wake up and meet your days with a sense of spiritual adventure. Meet each person who touches your life as a clue to the puzzle of this life you have made. Each one can give you a piece of information about yourself if you look closely enough. Without all the pieces your puzzle and your life will never be complete.

Change (Personal)

Here I am at our open door awaiting
your words to fill this space . . .

So many experiences you are having right now in your life are
giving you clues about how life works. You are watching your
spouse deal with the eminent demise of a dear friend with all
the sorrow, pain and anger that experience reveals. You are
watching friends try to change the path their life has taken thus
far, and seeing them question where they are and how they got
there and how to pull themselves out of what they perceive as a
stuck position. You have tried to remain neutral and loving but
have felt their pain, as a friend and soul partner should. All of
these life experiences are emotionally difficult and draining,
but they each serve a purpose. In any life path there are many
crossroads, choices that are made with the information available
at the time the crossroad appears. There are no wrong choices,
there are only the choices you make and the experiences those
choices give you. When a soul realizes they have learned all
they can from one choice or experience, that choice becomes
wearing on them, it pushes them to pull out of that choice, to
change their path as it were and take a different road. Changing
directions sounds easy, because you are used to doing it in
a vehicle or on foot, and that doesn't take much effort. But
changing direction on a life path is much different, it requires
a consistency of choice, it is not just a mental switch, changing
requires the mind, the body, the spirit and the energy to be
in perfect harmony to make that switch in order for it to work
effectively. You may say to yourself "I can't do this anymore"
and so decide that there is something else you would rather
do. But just frustration at a current situation and the voicing
of that frustration will never succeed in changing your path.

You need to know why this current path is not working for you, what you have learned from it about yourself and what the experience has taught you. You need to see far enough ahead to determine what it is you now wish to experience, and what gifts and talents you have to bring to the new endeavor. That is all mental and emotional. The last, and most important thing, is getting in touch with your spirit and switching your spiritual energy to coincide with your new direction and focus. With that mastered you let go. Your focus and intention is now solid and the universe will assist you in changing your direction. If this sounds like too much work, then you are not ready to change your path. There is nothing wrong with that, just be aware of it and take one day at a time until you are ready.

TREASURE HUNT

Here I am at our open door awaiting
your words to fill this space . . .

We wonder why it is so difficult for humans to grasp the idea
that all things are connected. Your scientists and ecologists
have proven time and again the interdependency of all
ecosystems in your world, but when it comes to recognizing
the interdependency of the human ecosystem there is very
little comprehension. The human being is just that, a soul
being human, living out a life it has chosen in order to gain
something by the experience. So each human walking your
earth is on the same general quest to gain or experience some
specific treasure. Yes, you could say each life is like a treasure
hunt. We see that this idea amuses you. But stop and think a
minute. A treasure hunt has a path laid out, with clues along
the way. Some clues are easy, some are more difficult. You can
take a path that will lead you off the course of the treasure,
and may have to adjust and backtrack to get back on the path
you want. At the end of the hunt you get to find what you
were searching for, so doesn't that sound like life? If each soul
inhabiting a body is on earth for the same basic reason, why
is there such a lack of understanding? Why is there this need
to accept and preserve this idea of individual sovereignty?
You don't stop to see each other and recognize that the same
struggles, emotions and despair you are feeling are echoed
in each person you pass. Each life that touches yours is an
echo of all your joy and sorrow. Open your eyes and heart to
that truth and life as you know it will change measurably for
the better. For when you realize the unifying power of your
goals, the echoes become voices raised in harmony together
to create the beautiful sound of lives lived on purpose.

LOOKING/SEEING

Here I am at our open door awaiting
your words to fill this space . . .

What do you see when you look at another person? Have you been trained to see anything? Have you ever thought about this? Your interaction with anyone else is almost totally based in an exchange of energy. But only a very small percentage of people understand this concept. It is not what a person looks like or what they are wearing, or what they sound like that attracts or repels you, it is their energy. This exchange of energy or the ability to feel and analyze the energy emitted by someone else is at the core of all interpersonal transactions. You come into this life path of yours preprogrammed to be attracted to or repelled by certain kinds of energy. You may not like that statement but it is true. You have all had the experience of an instant attraction to someone you have just met, likewise you have felt an instant aversion to another person you have just met. Why; because that is what you programmed for this life path. So those souls who have an active part in your life are there with a purpose. Wouldn't it be interesting to focus on that idea with each person in your life and really find out why you chose them? Your life is filled with immediate needs, chores, and responsibilities, we understand that. The idea of each person in your life being there for a reason may be hard to swallow, but if you can take an unbiased look at each relationship it may be possible for you to see with the eyes of your soul many aspects you have missed simply because your soul focus was never aimed at this particular idea. You may be amazed at what you find.

THE PAIN OF YOUR PLANET

Here I am at our open door awaiting
your words to fill this space . . .

We watch from the realm of energy and spirit as your societies
make their decisions regarding their reactions to events in your
world and we wonder how it is that you have allowed yourselves
to forget so much. You have forgotten that what hurts one
person hurts all. You have forgotten that your choice to be
where you are at this specific point in time was YOUR choice,
and so you have also forgotten that this global situation is one
in which you are very much a part. You may not wield the power
to make the large scale choice of becoming involved in another
nation's crisis. You may not be able to effect decisions being
made about global economic policy or global humanitarian
assistance. But you are capable of affecting the global situation
from right where you are. As we have said many times before
your world at its very core is based on the interlinking of energy.
It could be said that this energy makes your world go round.
So your job, if you can do nothing else, is to add your energy to
the collective consciousness of your planet for the benefit of all
who are suffering, all who are displaced and all who are without
the resources needed to sustain them. Your energy and focus
on the positive outcome in each of these areas will add to the
global energy to correct these out of balance situations. Being
angry and frustrated or feeling helpless is all negative energy,
it does not help anything. You must focus the most important
tool you have like the pinpoint of a laser onto the balancing
of your worldwide energy, so that the areas of concern to you
can be healed. Your world doesn't understand nor does it give
credence to this idea. But this is more important than you will
be able to comprehend as a global society for decades to come.

Have faith in what we tell you. What you call prayer is simply the focusing of your energy toward the energy of like-minded souls around your earth. That ribbon of golden energy builds as more and more of you add to it. It is that ribbon of energy that has the power to heal and put to rights all the anguish you see in these difficult times. Please add your efforts to those souls who have, will and do put their focus and their God given energies into healing the pain of your planet.

NEGATIVE ENERGY

Here I am at our open door awaiting
your words to fill this space . . .

One of the most difficult concepts for a soul in a human body
to learn is where your circle of influence and action ends and
where someone else's circle begins. Frustration and anger build
and spew over when we are trying to control someone else's
response to a given situation. We have said this before and will
most probably say it many times in the future, because it is so
important. Whatever your plan or goal is you must focus on it
and give it all the positive energy and movement you possibly
can. Then you must let go. Trying to get others to fall in with
our plans is fine, but just putting the idea out to others is
sufficient. They must make their own choices, just as you did.
Pushing and arguing only serve to add negative energy to your
goal. Negative energy is like the brakes on your car, it stops all
forward motion. It is to be avoided as much as humanly possible.
This is a very basic truth. Learn it and it will be so much easier
to live your life and walk your path. Ignore it and you will find
your life filled with emotional upheaval, frustration, anger and
sadness. It is such a simple concept yet one that is very difficult
for humans to master. You do control your life and your life
choices, you do not control anyone else, nor should you try to
do so. Sitting in judgment of others is another activity to be
avoided; you have your hands full with your own life, let that be
enough for you to handle. Others are making their way just as
you are; fighting their personal battles every day, just as you are.
Remember this when you come in contact with another soul.
Remember and bless their journey, then continue on your own.

ENERGY/FOCUS

Here I am at our open door awaiting
your words to fill this space . . .

Linear time is not something we deal with in the realm of
energy. We work with souls who have chosen a life path and
have inhabited a physical body. We have a strong energetic
connection to you, as other groups have to other humans. We
realize that you feel limited to the linear time frame in which
you live. That idea is not strictly true, but it is what you have
been taught and what your science propounds therefore it
has become your belief. When humankind has learned to use
more of its physical brain than it currently does it will realize
that there is nothing you cannot do. The tip of that iceberg
of learning to use more of your brain begins with energy and
focus, as we have said and will keep saying. Where your attention
lies is where your energy and focus are, your attention decides
what you will reap. Please try to understand we have no wish to
lecture you, only a wish to convey a basic truth, a very important
basic truth. We understand the very human need to want to
control something in a world that seems to be running amok.
But you try to control all the wrong things. You try to control
time and that is impossible, you try to control how others think
and act, and that is dishonoring of them and of yourself. Honor
the right of each person to make their own choices and have
their own opinions, just as you have yours. You rerun the past
in your heads as though by doing so you could change the
outcome, you can't. Learn whatever lesson you may need to
from the past and let it go. The present day, the present moment
is the only place you can make a difference. Why waste it on
that which you do not control. This moment, right now, is the
most precious thing you own, if you choose to own it. Here is

where your life is, here is where all your choices brought you and here is the only place you have immediate and everlasting control; <u>you</u> <u>in this</u> <u>moment</u>. Each of these moments is like a birth, a birth of choice. You can choose to waste it worrying about the past or the future, or you can live in it and endow it with your being, your energy and your intention. Making the choice to live in the moment makes your life path so much easier to walk, it makes it easier to understand, and easier to see clearly. Whatever your choice we will always be here walking with you and wishing you God's speed on your journey.

JUSTICE AND BALANCE

Here I am at our open door awaiting
your words to fill this space . . .

We are here tonight to speak of justice. Justice in your world
is rendered mostly under the rule of law. Energetically in the
spirit realm it is rendered by the cosmic consciousness, by
understanding that the experience of being the master must
be balanced by being the slave. So in order to understand
the ego and master the physical body you need to have lived
in the abuse of both, and the honoring of both. Everything
here is based on the balancing of all of our experiences in
body, and all of the energy that permeates our soul. We have
a vested interest in the physical lives of those we walk with
because we were there at the conception of that life path.
We watch and assist when invited to do so, and when we can.
The balancing of each soul is an integral part of the soul's
journey. Souls that are out of balance are in conflict with
the cosmic consciousness, and thus are in need of assistance
and direction in order to regain their balance. All of us move
toward the same ultimate goal. All of us must be in total
concert with each other in order to advance through this
world of energy. This is a major cooperative effort comprised
of love, understanding, acceptance, patience, guidance, and
ultimately advancement toward our desired completion.
We will speak more of this later. But it is important that you
understand that even though we exist here in a world of energy,
and you exist, for the moment, in the physical world, we are
working toward the same end. We are involved in your life
path whether you believe in us or not, whether you look to us
for assistance or not, whether you meet the goals you have set
on your life path or not, we will always be here for you. That

concept may be uncomfortable for some and inspiring for others, but whatever your reaction to that truth—we are here. You are never alone, and need never feel alone, reach inside yourselves and you will find the link that leads you to us.

CLEARING YOUR VISION

Here I am at our open door awaiting
your words to fill this space . . .

It is difficult to connect tonight. You need to take time to clear
your energy . . . . We will speak tonight of negative emotions
since that is what is uppermost in your mind and you cannot
seem to clear it. Life paths are beset with situations which
will try the patience of each soul. These are not arbitrary
situations they are, for the most part, a product of the choices
made throughout your life. Therefore there is something to be
learned from each incident that seems to you to be a trial. Many
souls relive the same situation repeatedly because they are not
willing to look at it clearly and dispassionately to determine
what is really being presented to them. When the passion of
anger, frustration and fear get a grip on your mind and heart
it is nearly impossible to see past it to the truth of a situation.
Unfortunately in order to clearly see the truth you have to wade
through the drama and emotion you feel. Until that energy
has been cleared you will be blinded by the negativity you are
swimming in mentally and emotionally. Knowing the tools that
will help you dispense with these overwhelming emotions is
half the battle. The other half is having the presence of mind
to use them. More often than not you will choose to take your
anger and frustration out on a loved one who doesn't deserve to
be dishonored in such a way. People do that to each other with
amazing frequency and it only serves to tear at the fabric of the
relationship. It would be far more sensible to use your spiritual
tools to dissipate the anger or frustration; then work with your
loved one to find a positive way to look at the issue of concern.
The best tools are an active type of meditation (because anger,
fear or frustration need activity to dissipate their energy),

a strong visualization format which will allow you to make a visual picture of what you are feeling and break it down into understandable pieces that you can then wrap positive thought and action around to dissipate them, or a private place where you can let loose the anger, fear or frustration without abusing anyone you love. Any of these tools can be very effective if you will stop for a moment and "get a grip" on that runaway feeling long enough to take yourself in hand and be constructive with your feelings of helplessness. Without using these tools you run the risk of damaging your relationships, perhaps beyond repair. That is not a choice we would like to see you make. Relationships you have chosen on your life path are there for very good reason and should be handled with the greatest of care because they are the greatest of gifts.

PEACEFUL MOMENTS

Here I am at our open door awaiting
your words to fill this space . . .

Does anyone in your world speak of Peace anymore? As we
watch we see so much activity, so much frenzy, so much that
you feel needs to be accomplished in each of your days. But
where is the enjoyment of a peaceful moment? Your life path
is just that a life path, and similar to every other path you have
ever taken. When you walk through the woods, or walk on a
beach, is it only to get the exercise over with so you can move
on to your next chore; or do you actually pause to see what
surrounds you? Do you fill your senses with the sights, sounds
and smells of your environment; or are you only using your
sense of urgency to get through to the next task on your list. We
would encourage you to think of each of your days as a walk on
the beach or a stroll through the woods. We would encourage
you to fully engage all of your senses in each of your days. That
way you will not miss any of the miracles out there waiting for
you. You won't miss the tired eyes of someone whose soul only
needs the touch of your smile to give them the energy they
need to keep on coping. You won't miss the encouraging look
of a friend or coworker when you need it most. You won't miss
the beauty of the sky or the sound of birdsong that can lighten
your heart if you will allow it to do so. Rushing through each
of your days does an injustice to your soul and the magnificent
world in which you live. You miss the miracle of opportunity
that each new day brings. When you talk about your days you
sometimes use the phrase "I spent my day . . . . .", and that is
exactly what you did. But what did you purchase with what
you spent; a feeling of fatigue, or gratitude that it is over and
behind you, or regret over a mistake or an argument? Wouldn't

it be wonderful to have spent your day and ended up with the purchase of a special smile that came unexpectedly, or the sound of a laughing child you passed on your way to lunch, or with a look of understanding from a stranger. Finding a place of peace in each of your days is essential to making the most of them; making each of them a spiritual part of your life path; not time to get through until you reach some nebulous future goal. We encourage you to find a point of peace in each of your days, something you can point to at the end of each day and say "There is where I saw my soul today, and there I was at peace."

TRUE FRIENDSHIP

Here I am at our open door awaiting
your words to fill this space . . .

Our subject tonight is "True Friendship". Most of what passes
for friendship in your world hardly deserves to be called by that
name. It is, more often than not, simply a relationship fostered
by proximity. At its worst it can be harmful and dishonoring.
When two people meet and speak to each other but do not take
the time to listen, when they just take turns speaking, or worse,
listen only enough to find something to criticize, this is not
friendship. At best you have an acquaintance, at worse a budding
enemy. True friendship does not judge, nor does it criticize. It is
a balm to the spirit of both, and a salve to the wounded of heart
and mind. It is a safe haven for your anxieties to be spoken aloud
without fear of judgment or criticism. It is a place for your heart
and mind to find solace and safety. Being a true friend is not a
job for the faint of heart. To be a true friend is a soul calling out
to another soul. It is a commitment of time, attention, love and
understanding. It encourages and bolsters a faint heart in times
of trouble and stress, and is there to celebrate the triumphs of
spirit that can only be shared with those of like mind. Friendship
is no simple thing. It takes a gentle, loving heart, and a clear
vision uncluttered by the vagaries of physical life. Search your
mind and heart and see if you have true friends, or if you are
one to anyone. That is the test of how much of your soul you
are expressing here on your life path. Touching another soul
with your true friendship brings blessings to both of you.

COURAGE

Here I am at our open door awaiting
your words to fill this space . . .

We will speak of our understanding of the word courage tonight. Your world seems to give the word a meaning that encompasses some form of physical might and mental toughness that aids in conquering overwhelming odds. That is all well and good, but for us the word signifies a strength of character that is constant in its tenacity. To us it is the willingness to get up each day and enter your physical life without a mask. It is the enduring quality that takes each day and brings to it the eyes that see the souls that surround you, not just the masks they wear. It is the quietness of heart that emits loving energy to any soul in need. This is the intrinsic energy of a soul driven life. This is what we see in a life in which the soul inside the physical body has taken control and despite all physical appearances to the contrary, believes and lives its "soul" purpose, open of mind and heart to the moment by moment events of each day. Bringing to the table all of the souls' bright pleasure in just being, sharing, experiencing and loving. This is courage of the highest order from our viewpoint. Admittedly we are not currently experiencing physical form, and cannot truly judge how difficult it may be on various life paths to live with this kind of courage. But know that courage like this is possible and an option for each and every soul in human form. It is not only optional, it is what you wished to be able to achieve when you set out your life path. Think about this when you wake in the morning. Think about trying to achieve it even if only for a few minutes each day. See how it feels to be truly you in all of your soul glory. It is after all what you were created to be.

THE POWER OF PRAYER

I am here at our open door awaiting
your words to fill this space . . .

We wish to speak of the power of Prayer. As we have stated
many times in these messages the real power each human
has is in how they focus their energy and intention. Prayer is
a perfect example of that focusing of energy and intention.
The prayers you are taught in many of your world's religions
are memorized and many times are repeated without thought.
They seem to be syllables strung together with little meaning
or focus. When you pray make the prayer your own; whether it
is a prayer you have been saying since childhood or an original
prayer from your heart. Make it meaningful to your life, and
instill your energy, focus and intention into it. In this way you
invest your soul's power into that prayer. Personal prayers are
the most effective prayers an individual soul can offer. They
are invested with your heart and your love. They have great
power. Group prayer is another power-filled way to affect the
outcome of situations on your earth. Many people of like mind
and intention, praying the same prayer, investing that prayer
with their hearts concern and purpose are using the gift of
their soul focus to bring forth their heart's desire. These are
excellent ways in which to practice the art of focusing your
intention and energy. Praying isn't something you just do in
your many and varied houses of worship, it can be done at any
time of the day or night in any surroundings. All it takes is a
wish to communicate to something larger than yourself or the
circumstances in your life. It can be a thank you, a request,
or an apology. It can be whatever you need it to be, as long
as it comes through your heart and from your soul. We wish
to extend the invitation to practice praying each day. Make

it part of who you are and you will be amazed at how much stronger you feel, and how much the physical world around you becomes more in tune with the idea of what you mean your life to be. We are always listening, watching and waiting for soul felt prayers to be sent forth on their journey of creation.

LIGHT

Here I am at our open door awaiting
your words to fill this space . . .

Tonight our topic is light. This may strike you as a strange topic
but it is a very basic idea on which to build a life. Light can mean
many things in your world. It can mean the easing of some
burden, it can mean having a visually illuminated area in which
to see what is around you; light can mean to strike a match.
For our purposes however the Light of which we speak is the
Light that comes from within. The glow of spirit that makes life
easier to understand, makes others easier to empathize with,
and makes it possible for you to know the other souls in your
life at their soul level. This is the Light of your spirit. The Light
you brought into this world when you embarked upon your life
path. It is the Light that is exclusively yours and yours alone.
No two souls radiate this Light in exactly the same way, just as
in your world no two fingerprints are exactly the same. This
light, when you are in touch with it, can radiate through every
situation in your life and bring it peace. We don't mean that this
Light can magically change others in a situation; that is not it
at all. But when you are in this Light of yours, your perception
of all the situations around you shifts so subtly that the clarity
of vision gives you the ability to see the peace in any human
puzzle. This Light is transformative and all encompassing. It
clarifies your mind and brings to your life an ability to accept
that which you cannot change in any particular situation or
person. Finding that Light within yourself and living in that
Light is one of the most soul enhancing tasks you can set for
yourself. But to find it and then live in it you must first be willing
and able to go inside yourself. To figuratively enter your own
head and heart and look for the key that opens the door to this

Light. That key is your willingness to live trusting in something bigger than yourself. To be steadfast in the knowledge of your connection to something larger than you. Being able to cling to that truth opens the door and allows the Light to play freely over your soul, your physical self and your physical life. Achieve that and your life will be a daily experience of clarity of purpose and understanding. Physical life in your world without this Light can become what you would term a hell on earth.

LAUGHTER

Here I am at our open door awaiting
your words to fill this space . . .

Pure, joyous laughter is one of the most healing energies on
your planet. It can take a heavy heart and fill it with light. It
can strengthen a bond that was unraveling between two souls.
It can unite enemies and build friendships. This one simple
emotion can transcend barriers of race, faith, nationality and
gender. Used in constructive and honoring ways it is the most
effective and least harmful of any energy or weapon in the
arsenal of man. Your humorists and comedians are, for the
most part, a creative and artful group of people who, when
using their craft creatively and in an honoring fashion, show
the hilarity of the foibles of human beings. All mankind can
relate to this kind of humor and join in the laughter. There
are actual physical changes in the human body when honest
and joy-filled laughter occurs. This is something your science
already knows. So when the opportunity arises, give in to the
joy of laughter. It is so good for the soul. Your lives are filled
with enough responsibility, work, drama, chaos, and world
news to overflow your days. Build up the boundaries around
yourself with a healthy wall of laughter, the healing energy.

SPRING ENERGY

Here I am at our open door awaiting
your words to fill this space . . .

You on earth are well into your rejuvenation season. Spring is
the reviving season for all things. What very few of you realize
is that as the plant life and all species emerge from winter so
does the earth itself. What we mean is the energy of the earth
rises as well as the energy levels in all living things. This increase
in energy, all the energy that surrounds you, has a definite
impact on each human being. During this time of year your
dreams become more vivid and more frequently memorable.
There is a reason for this. Those who walk with each of you
are trying to communicate with you about those areas in your
life where you need to be watchful. Learning how to interpret
your dreams is a tool that can be used with great success.
Realizing that this increase in energy is happening to everyone
is something to keep in mind as you go about your day. You will
note that there is much more drama in the lives of your friends
and acquaintances than usual, and perhaps in your own life as
well. Being aware is great, but knowing what you need to do to
stay centered as all of this energetic turmoil surrounds you is
essential. The best tools to use are meditation and visualization.
We have spoken of meditation before, and there are many kinds,
from the simplistic to the complex. It doesn't matter which one
works for you just be sure to use it on a daily basis if possible.
Don't get lazy about it or you will end up caught in the dramas
swirling around you. Visualizations are a quick and wonderful
tool and very effective for controlling excess or invasive energy.
Visualizing a vacuum hose from the center of the earth pulling
all the unwanted energy out of your energy field is very effective.
Everyone knows what a vacuum sounds like so it becomes a very

effective tool. The sound of a flushing toilet can be another effective tool to use to get rid of an unwanted excess of energy. Staying clear and clean of everyone else's turmoil is not an easy task, especially during spring, because everyone seems so willing to share the disasters they perceive in their lives. You can listen and be supportive just don't get pulled into their perceptions of their lives. Each soul must make their decisions and their choices on their own. Lending an ear is one thing, becoming embroiled is another. Encourage your friends to do what they feel is best for themselves and remind them of their strengths. You need to do that for yourself as well. The energy of spring will eventually settle down and so will most of the dramas now playing themselves out in your world. Just hold on tightly to the bright soul that lives in you and you will make it through this upheaval with as much growth and as little pain as possible. And always remember you have a host of energies that walk with you ready to give you support. We are always here.

THE POWER OF AN IDEA

Here I am at our open door awaiting
your words to fill this space . . .

There is chaos in your world right now on a global level. This combined with the energy of spring has taken the upheaval and the conflicts to new heights. Many nations are struggling for the freedom to have open and honest governments that are fair to all. All of these changes are energy driven. It starts with the energy which creates an idea; the idea creates a product—like the computer, which in turn ends up creating the World Wide Web. This creation spreads ideas across your world in the flash of an instant; ideas that have never seen the light of day in some parts of your globe. These ideas spark thought and that thought sparks action; hence the turmoil that is spreading through the Middle East. All of this started by the simple energy of an idea. It is strange that your world thinks its weapons of war are so daunting, when it is really the energy in an idea which holds the real power to create change. Your world, for the most part, has lost its belief in the power of an idea. It is focused on gain, on amassing wealth. While 2/3rds of your world lives in mass poverty on virtually every continent, most of those with the power and money to create solutions to this inequity are focused on amassing more wealth. There must be a shift in the consciousness of your planet if real change is to have a chance. That shift begins with you, in your thoughts, in your interactions with others, and in where you hold your focus. Every person wherever they stand in your world can make an enormous difference if they will shift their thoughts from just surviving to thoughts of appreciation, of caring for, of helping out. If each of you does this in greater and greater numbers there will be a quantum shift in your global consciousness. When that shift happens, miracles happen. People become more important than things, ideas become more important than weapons, and spirit becomes more important than ego. This is how you help your fellow travelers on this journey and this is how you change your world. One energized idea and focus at a time.

PERCEIVED INJUSTICE

Here I am at our open door awaiting
your words to fill this space . . .

Our topic tonight is perceived injustice. We are not talking
about gross injustice on a large scale. Not about what happens
between ethnic and religious groups, or between nations. We
are talking about interpersonal relationships, about people
you interact with every day, who to you, in some instances treat
you or your loved ones unjustly. This is what we wish to clarify.
When someone's attitude, words, or actions offend or upset you,
when you feel threatened, mistreated, undervalued or verbally
abused, it is time to stop . . . before reacting to the perceived
injustice, stop. Force your ego out of the way . . . we know this
is difficult for the soul in a human body to do, but if you are to
receive the blessing in the situation you must stop and set the
ego aside, so you can clear your vision and your ability to sense
what is actually happening. There is an opportunity in each
of these situations for each of the parties involved to receive
the blessing of clear vision and the gift of understanding what
is really taking place. Taking the time to realize there is more
going on than what is on the surface of any given situation is the
most intelligent and soul directed choice you can make. This is
a difficult action for human beings to learn to do because you
are taught by example to react to stimuli rather than acting
upon stimuli. So it takes time to retrain yourselves to shift your
natural response to a more thoughtful and soul felt approach.
If more of you are able to learn this, and make it a part of who
you are and how you see the world and each of its situations
you would save yourselves a great deal of frustration, anger,
time and resentment. Learning to see and hear with more than
just the physical senses is an attribute that will enhance your

life and the lives of all of those around you for the rest of your journey. We encourage you to take the time and exercise the restraint necessary to learn this new approach. We encourage you to set the example in this for your family and friends and by doing so you will enrich your portion of the world.

GUIDELINES

Here I am at our open door awaiting
your words to fill this space . . .

Sharon, you know the value of meditation. You meditated
daily for decades and it gave you many healthful benefits. We
would encourage you to start the practice again. What we
do here each day cannot take the place of pure meditation.
Our meetings with you are simply to give you information to
transcribe in the hopes that others in your world will benefit
from these words. Each of these meetings produces one piece of
information from our point of view. Information that we want
very much to share with any who are interested enough to take
the time to read and try to understand. Each of these pages
bears witness to some truth from this side. Some of these truths
are being reiterated because it is of primary importance to us
that you understand what we are trying to make clear. From
this side we can only do so much. We need permission which
then provides an opening into your world in order to convey
something more, or affect the outcome of some event for which
you are seeking assistance. Please be aware that we are never
to interfere in your lives without your prayer asking for help, or
your openness of heart and soul inviting our companionship as
you walk your life path. These are the basic rules, the guidelines
we must follow when walking with our loved ones who have
chosen to return to the physical world. Most of us spend much
of the time following a soul in physical form without ever being
acknowledged. That is the way some lifetimes are set up. But
we must let you know that those lifetimes are very troubling to
watch. We are aware when we accept that role that watching
and having no real contact is giving us the chance to bless
the progress of the soul we are bound to, but cannot assist.

Assistance or the lack of assistance is decided by the soul when setting up their life journey. Watching over you is our sacred trust, an honor that is taken very seriously simply because all of us ultimately are ONE. No one goes up the mountain by themselves. As we have said before we are all in this journey of discovery together, so helping to make your pathway clearer or give insight where needed is something that delights each of us.

Resistance

Here I am at our open door awaiting
your words to fill this space . . .

We wish to speak of resistance now. You have a perfect saying in
your world, "What you resist; persists". That is very accurate. But
why is it accurate? Have you ever noticed that a stream of water
never stops to push against the rocks in its path; it simply parts
and goes around them. This is a perfect analogy for the way
spirit should react to an obstacle put in its path. Butting heads
and getting angry over some obstacle or opinion that seems
to be blocking your path is a waste of energy and time. Simply
learn to observe, listen, assess, and take in the full picture of
what is being presented to you. Then see with your soul's eyes
what is beneath the entire situation. Most of the time what you
will find is ego. One ego fighting another for dominance, for the
right to direct the actions of others where there is no consensus.
When this happens try to calmly speak your piece, and go your
own way. This will often mean separating yourself from a group
you may really want to be a part of, but if you are listening to
spirit, then this is a group that will not honor who you are or
where you are going. There is nothing wrong in stepping away,
although you may find your path lonely for a time, this is better
than being in a group that will be forever butting heads and
creating dramas for the chance to educate themselves. Being a
part of these groups or getting involved in situations filled with
conflict serves no purpose for you unless there is something for
you to learn from the experience. In some instances you may
choose to remain a part of the situation or group simply because
you need the experience of speaking up for your point of view,
or helping a weaker soul find their strength of will to steer clear
of these situations. But whatever the reason make sure you

are true to who you are in all encounters in your life. For the most part people will take the path of least resistance, in other words, they will go along with the majority of the group so they don't make waves, or to avoid focusing attention to them. Or conversely they will argue and get angry because no one in the group will side with them. Both of these actions are undertaken by souls with something to learn from the encounter. An older soul will stop, make an assessment of the situation with their heart and soul, then most likely turn around and leave. As we have said, doing this can put you on a lonely road for a while, but it also can guarantee you peace of mind that cannot be found in conflict, argument, and playing for power over others.

SHOWING UP

Here I am at our open door awaiting
your words to fill this space . . .

What happened to the peacefulness of just being? What happened to taking simple joy in completing a chore or in the actual work in getting the chore done? As we have noted before the overwhelming energy on your planet seems to be turning more and more frenetic. Humans need to be connected and entertained all of their waking hours. There seem to be very few of you who find joy in simply being. In fact to most of you that would be an idiotic statement. We understand that the innovation explosion has created more and better and faster ways to stay in touch with each other and connected to your world. But are you aware that the connection is not a personal one? The connection, the being in touch with, is all electronic. Most of you would rather text a message than talk to someone.

Face to face communication is becoming very rare. You are rarely using your verbal skills and almost never using your other perceptive skills. When was the last time you really had a face to face, heart to heart conversation with anyone? We realize that in order to function successfully in your world you must use the communication devices available to you, and "Go with the flow", so to speak. But in doing so please remember that as a soul in a human body your primary quest is to touch each person who appears in your life with the Light of your spirit. You cannot achieve this goal through telecommunications. It must be a face to face, person to person, heart to heart experience. But this, just like everything else in your life, is a choice that only you can make. Please realize that the life path you set out for yourself will always connect you to the souls you were meant to meet here, only you can choose whether you will show up in person or not.

WORSHIP

Here I am at our open door awaiting
your word to fill this space . . .

We have spoken here very candidly and openly about the choosing of life paths and about the implementing of those choices. We know that for many in your world this concept is not only foreign but absurd. We understand the thinking that goes into that mindset and we honor the souls who feel that the information we are sending is a fabrication. You each must choose for yourselves what feels right to you and those choices must be honored because each of you has every right to make them—for yourselves—you cannot make this choice of belief for anyone else. However, many, many people and groups in your world try to do so. Belief is meant to be a personal powerhouse for each individual soul. But more often than not it becomes a source of power over groups of people, many times power over millions of people. Please understand that this is not a criticism, it is merely a statement of what we observe. Organized religion would not exist if people didn't need it in their lives. However, such power over masses of people brings with it tremendous responsibility. A responsibility to honor all of those who look to you for spiritual guidance, a responsibility to never abuse the trust placed in you, and to live the precepts of your belief to the fullest extent possible in human form. These guidelines for religious leaders should be easily understood in each and every one of your religions, because they refer back to the tenets of love, honor, charity, honesty and peace that are the foundations for all of your faiths. We earnestly encourage you each to find such a place of worship if that is your heart's desire. But understand also that not all souls inhabiting a human body need a building and a group of like-minded people in order to worship or express their soul's joy. Many need only to look at the sky, or see the beauty in a tree, or look in the eyes of a beloved pet in order to feel the link to their creator. Worship can be done in so many ways. It is good to remember that each of you is unique and so too are the ways in which you choose to express your joy in life and your connection to your creator. You are all the children of that initial Creative Energy Force.

CONFLICT

Here I am at our open door awaiting
your words to fill this space . . .

The energy level in your world right now is extraordinarily high
so we would like to give you a tool to help you center yourself
when your world seems to be in chaos. We know that it is an
almost mindless reaction to jump right into drama whenever it
presents itself. However, this reaction does nothing to resolve
the issue at hand. Adding your own energy to an already volatile
situation is a very bad mix. We suggest that instead you step
back literally and figuratively, and separate yourself from the
drama playing out before you. When you step back we ask that
you focus your attention on the center of your forehead. This
is what your eastern religions call the "third eye". Allow your
energy to pour over the situation from this area of the forehead,
and keep yourself removed from the area of conflict. In a short
period of time you should be able to see a clear indication of
what is truly happening before you. It is rarely what is being
discussed. At this point, if you feel you can add something to the
conversation that will address the real issues, please do so, but
remain on the edges of the conflict. With any luck at all you will
be able to diffuse the confrontation. But even if you can't you
will have added something that no one else could see. This tool
should work in any kind of verbal assault situation, but it may
take a few tries to perfect it. Keep at it and you will succeed.

LOOKING FOR THE LIGHT

Here I am at our open door awaiting
your words to fill this space . . .

Your main goal in these chaotic energy times is simply to find
the light in each of your days. You know what light is; it is the joy,
the laughter, the love, the sense of rightness in your life. Many of
you will look at your lives and say that you see very little of these
things. If that is the case you are not looking with the right eyes.
It takes the eyes of your soul as well as your physical eyes to see
all the light in your life. Learning to look with the eyes of your
soul is not something that the customs and expectations of your
world allows you the time to do, so you must take the time. If you
are feeling worn down, troubled, listless, and without passion for
anything in your life, you are responsible for finding your way
back to the light. No one can do it for you. You can reach out
to those on your path, but they may be dealing with their own
troubles and be unable to see yours. The best thing to do is go
within, find the Light God placed in you, connect with that again,
it will renew you. Speak to your soul self and those who walk
with you will be overjoyed that you are connected to them again.
They can help you refocus and renew your perspective and your
passion for why you are here. They can help you identify why you
returned and what you can do to shift your perspective and see
more clearly the world around you. This is not an easy task, it is
far easier to stay stuck and drift along in the dusk of your life. But
finding the courage to search for the Light is what your soul is
crying for or you would not have notice that something is missing.
Please take that look inside and find the wonder that all of us on
this side see every day. See with our eyes and you will never ever
give up on yourself or on anyone else. We walk with you to bless
your journey, give us the chance to serve our purpose in your life.

PATIENCE

Here I am at our open door awaiting
your words to fill this space . . .

Patience is not something used very often in your world.
Yours is a world that is more and more addicted to instant
gratification. But in each relationship the one quality that is
overlooked the most is patience. You may see what you perceive
to be a lack in your spouse, or some failure in a friend, and
immediately you want to address the issue. But you would be
far wiser to wait for the opening to present itself where you
are asked for your help or opinion. Once asked, the other
soul is offering you a way into their heart. If you take that
opportunity by allowing your soul self to lead the way, you can
be a blessing to the situation rather than sit in judgment of it.
Patience and perspective are two underutilized qualities. It is
so easy to see and judge almost in the same instant, instead
of seeing and stepping back so that your heart and soul can
assess what is really happening. Humans in general seem to
have little or no compunction about judging before they have
even given a clear moment of thought to a situation. Perhaps
this is the result of the multitasking behavior that you have
all been made to believe is the only way in which you can
live your lives efficiently. Whatever the reason, making snap
judgments without giving each situation your total attention is
dishonoring of who you are and of all of those souls involved
in a situation. We have said this before using different words
and scenarios, but the message is the same. Slow down, stop
when necessary, and use all of who you are each day in each
of your encounters with another soul. Don't miss the miracles
that await you when you truly see another person. Don't
miss the opportunity to let your internal light and gift shine

within each of your days. These are the reasons you chose to return. Don't let even one day go by without endowing it with the light of who you really are, and filling it with the unique understanding only your soul can bring to any situation.

PIECES FALLING INTO PLACE (PERSONAL)

Here I am at our open door awaiting
your words to fill this space . . .

You have been pleasantly surprised today at how many of the
pieces have suddenly fallen into place. But you were the catalyst
for all of it. When you listened to our request that you let go and
allow the other souls on your life path to make their choices,
you also allowed universe to assist in making those choices easy.
This is a perfect example of how life is able to work when you
focus only on the intent you have and do everything you can
with your own life and choices to reach that end. There is no
need to worry about the choices others will make; that is up
to them. Be content with making your own and having faith
in the process. So much can be accomplished by just letting
go, and so few people realize it. Letting go releases the stress
and worry that tie you up in knots and accomplish nothing
else. Letting go clears your mind of concerns over things you
cannot control. And letting go allows you to use your personal
energy constructively by moving you forward toward your goal
without the impediment of trying to be the puppet master.
We know that this is a difficult concept to grasp and master.
But the sooner you use it and become accustom to allowing
all souls in your life the freedom to choose for themselves the
sooner your freedom to live your life on your terms becomes
complete. We know this current situation will be a good
example of how this process works and that you will remember
it and proceed accordingly with all the other situations in your
life. We are happy to have been here for you this time, and
will be here to assist in any capacity we can in the future.

SELFLESSNESS

Here I am at our open door awaiting
your words to fill this space . . .

We will speak of selflessness tonight. For humans this usually conjures up pictures of people who commit all of themselves and their resources to a cause or a person leaving next to nothing for themselves. That is not the selflessness we will define here. Our selflessness is one of moving the ego out of the way and leaving room for the soul to take control of your direction. It is removing the ego SELF and finding the connection to a higher path that eludes most of mankind. This shift in perspective is what miracles are made of because it allows the soul-self freedom to reign as you walk your life path. Achieving this state of being is very difficult in your world because you are not given the time to assess what the benefits would be. Your world wears you out every day because you allow it to do so. You allow the energy of others to infect you and wonder why you are tired or sick or angry. In order to find this miracle you need to take control of your mind and heart and stop. Just stop for several minutes every day and focus on what you have in your life that brings you joy. Start there, and don't compare what you have that gives you joy to anyone else or anything else that you don't have. Just focus on your joy. Then do the same thing with peace. What in your life brings you peace? Find one thing that brings you peace and focus on it alone. Focusing on joy and peace may seem a silly task in a world that is filled with disasters, natural and otherwise, but the simple focusing of your energy on something positive in your life changes what and how you feel. Try it for just a few minutes each day. That really isn't too much of a chore when you remember that the ultimate goal is to bring you a miracle. As you learn to become accustomed to searching for the positive in your world you will notice subtle changes in how you are seeing others and in the situations that surround you. These changes will be small but positive, as though you are sifting through all the incoming data and seeing with more clarity because everyone else's energy is being removed from your picture. This is the miracle of selflessness, getting the ego self out of the way and training your mind to see with your soul's eye the clarity in each situation. This becomes a daily miracle for you because it allows your soul to be a major contributor to your physical life. There is no greater gift you can give yourself or those you walk with than the sunlight from your soul.

LETTING GO—AGAIN!
(PERSONAL)

Here I am at our open door awaiting
your words to fill this space . . .

We are delighted to see you arrive safely at your destination. This time away will serve many purposes and be good for all the souls involved. We have spoken often of "letting go" and this is a perfect way to practice that skill. It seems that each and every human being has this need to try to micromanage every aspect of their lives. That is such a waste of so much of your energy. Each person involved in your life has their own idea of what the perfect outcome of each and every situation should be, and none of them will be exactly the same as yours. So try to remember you are the only person you have control over. Don't tie your peace or happiness or contentment to what someone else deems appropriate for them in any given situation. "Letting go" of the outcome means taking hold of your purpose, and letting everyone else be responsible for their purpose. Yes, there are times when having others to depend on is important to you and your life, but you can't make their choices for them and when they choose not to show up in your life the way you need them to, you need to decide how that soul fits into your picture of reality, or if they still fit in your life at all. If they don't, bless them and send them on their way with love. You lose nothing by being gracious and you gain the peace of knowing that your soul has won over your ego self. These "soul versus ego" engagements are an ongoing part of the growth of a soul in a human body. We wish you success in your ongoing growth.

Barrick (Personal)

Here I am at our open door awaiting
you words to fill this space . . .

The tears you cry for the passing of your friend do honor to his
soul and his life. The people he touched were warmed by his
humor, educated by his intelligence and inspired by his strong
convictions. We rejoice as his soul returns home to us and he
enriches our energy. Those on this side who walked with Barrick
through his life walked in silence, as this lifetime of his did not
promote the spiritual connection. But his life was rich in its
connection to creation in many other ways. He loved to grow
things and there is no better way to rejoice in creation than that.
He was creative of mind and expressed his belief in the holistic
ways to heal the body. He had strong beliefs he held to firmly.
He was a staunch and steadfast friend. His life is to be celebrated
as a tribute to his soul because he completed his life path with
all its ups and down with an unflinching integrity of spirit. He
is well loved and his passing in your world will leave a hole in
the lives of many. This is the mark of a life well and truly lived.

HOME

Here I am at our open door awaiting
your words to fill this space . . .

Home is on your mind since you have just returned, so let
us use that as our topic tonight. Coming home means many
different things to those in your world. But from our vantage
point it is simply entering a space you have created for yourself
that is not only honoring of who you are, but surrounds you
with a fortifying energy that both protects the essential energy
of your soul and also feeds your ability to stay in contact with
your soul self. So Home is not just a roof over your head, it
is an oasis of peace and connectivity to that essential part of
yourself. Most of you who walk your Earth do not have this
type of Home. It takes truthful and vigilant seeking of self
to begin to create such a space. But once you have laid the
foundation for this oasis, finding the time and energy to make
it your Home becomes a driving force within you. There is no
safer place for you to be, and no place that will feed the soul
inside you more generously. Peace is to be found in this place
always, as are love, understanding, and the ability to honor all
of those who walk into your life. This Home is of more value
to your passage on your life path than any shelter contrived
in your physical world. Try to remember this when you get
caught up in the physical needs of your world. For sooner
or later each and every soul on Earth will need the Home
that is at the heart of your life path, the Home that is your
spiritual oasis. Build this Home and you will have all the rest
you need to sustain you on the life path you have chosen.

THE LINK

Here I am at our open door awaiting
your words to fill this space . . .

You care for your world the way you care for your souls, nearly not at all. This may sound harsh but it is only what we see from our vantage point. Your planet is being abused as you abuse the physical bodies your souls inhabit. These gifts were created for you to inhabit, enjoy, bless and revere; but somewhere along the way the key that unlocks the link between your soul, your body and your earth has been lost. The majority of you go about your day with no thought to why you are there, or even who you really are. You live in thoughts of the past, or of the future and very rarely of the now. Soon you will have to wake up to the realization that there is a purpose in every day of your life. There is a purpose to each encounter with another. You have total control over how you use each of your days, how you react to each situation presented, and whether or not you will appreciate each moment of the time you are spending there. That control comes at a price, and that price is that you will have the opportunity to review all of your choices when this life is done. Most souls are saddened by the loss of vision they exhibited when they were in body. They feel that most of their lives where spent with blinders on, as if just outside their line of sight there were miracles waiting to be noticed. Don't miss your chance to see the miracles around you. Take off the blinders of ego, resistance, anger, frustration, hurt, envy, and intolerance and open your soul's eyes to the beauty that surrounds you. This life was your choice, do not forget that. Own what you have chosen and become the creator of your life, not just the inhabitant of it. You have at your disposal all the help you need in those who walk with you. Get still and make the connection to your soul self, when you do your journey through this life will take on a new glow that will brighten all the corners that were shadowed.

Now

*Here I am at our open door awaiting
your words to fill this space . . .*

We have often heard you ask that people you include in your prayers find peace and joy in each of their days. This is a very spiritual wish. It is simple but carries with it the knowledge that finding peace and joy in each day means they are present in each of their days. This is a blessing we wish for every soul in human form, for it allows for an appreciation and understanding of what is happening in the Now. We have spoken many times about the need to hone your ability to stay in the present, and we will keep mentioning it until there is no longer a need for us to remind you. It would be impossible for us to stress this too strongly. The present is what you have at hand, it is what you have control over as far as what you think, say, and do right now. No one is promised the future and the past is over, so making the most of the Now is essential because that is the space in which you live. It is the only thing you can affect. It is truly the gift of opportunity, ever present in your life. Your life is contained in each passing moment, in each choice you make in each of those moments. Not being present in these moments is to abandon your life path to apathy, or worse to abandon it over regret for yesterday, or anxiety over tomorrow. No good can ever come of those things. Choose to be present in each moment of your day, choose to spend all of the moments of your day with a focus on the Now, and the rest of your life will be rewarded by it.

ENRICHING YOUR LIFE
WITH GRATITUDE

Here I am at our open door awaiting
your words to fill this space . . .

How often do you stop to notice your breath? Breathing keeps
your physical body alive yet it is not something you give a
moment's thought, until it is impaired in some way. If you stop
to think about it all of the gifts that are essential to human life
are similarly dismissed or neglected by most of you, until they
are threatened. By and large your human nature is to take for
granted all the gifts of life you have been given and to strive
for those you feel you need instead. It is a sad dance to watch
from our perspective. Comparatively few of the billions of
humans on earth find any joy or peace in each of their days.
This lack of awareness is always the most painful realization
when you return Home. The waste of time spent on things
that cannot be changed is another painful realization. So we
stress to you to live in awareness of who and what you are, see
your life, your surroundings, and your families with your soul's
eyes and appreciate what is in your life for all that it is. The
heart that continually beats in your chest, the limbs that do
your bidding each day, your senses that work in total harmony
with each other, all of these functions bless your life each and
every moment of every day. Don't ignore them or take them for
granted. Being grateful for each of these gifts brings a daily
awareness of the richness in each of your lives. Acknowledge
these gifts with your thanks each day and watch how your
appreciation enhances all of the other aspects of your life.

PAY ATTENTION

Here I am at our open door awaiting
your words to fill this space . . .

We have spoken frequently about being observant of your
surroundings. This also has the added benefit of keeping you
focused in the Now of your life. Awareness of your surroundings
doesn't just mean knowing where you are, it means paying
attention to the people and interaction going on around
you. There are an infinite number of insights you can absorb
just from watching closely the interplay of people, words and
emotions taking place. Pay attention to the way different people
use their energy. This is very important because you will learn
how to protect yourself from the energy of others. Being able
to identify, and neutralize an invasive energy is of paramount
importance in going about your daily life unscathed. The sooner
you can master this particular task the better off your body
will be. Please heed us when we say this, it is a very important
tool to have access to in moments of heavy stress. Being alert
to your surroundings is a positive and nonintrusive way to stay
on top of every change in your environment. It doesn't take
long to learn to use this energy awareness technique. Please
take this advice seriously; it will make your life so much easier.

RELAXATION

*Here I am at our open door awaiting
your words to fill this space . . .*

Now our topic is relaxation. For the majority of you work, home, chores and responsibilities fill your days to overflowing. Add to this the need to be connected to your world electronically all of your waking hours and you have no time at all to relax. We don't mean watching entertainment, whether it is computer generated or Television, we mean relaxation of mind, body and spirit. This is something the majority of you rarely, if ever, do. Some of you consider the time you spend exercising your bodies as your relaxation time, and to a certain extent that can be true. Physical exercise can lower stress levels and produce hormones to revive the body. But we would suggest that the clearing of the mind and heart are just as important, and that cannot be done without taking the time to pull away from all the demands of your life and find a space of peace and calm that can lighten your heart, cleanse your mind, and feed your soul. Meditation is the one thing that can provide this respite, and it is a gift you can give yourself that will serve you better than anything else your physical world can offer. We have spoken of this before and will probably revisit this issue again, for without the calm clarity provided by meditation you will spend your life fighting through a sea of emotional and energetic chaos. You may say that is just the way your world is and that you are used to the constant connection and the necessary multitasking, but all circuits overload in time and the human body, as miraculous an instrument as it is, is no different in this respect than any other mechanism. Please take heed when we tell you that to safeguard yourself and your purpose for being in your physical body, you would do well to consider giving meditation a try. What you will find will enrich your life and make the path you walk clearer and far more peaceful.

PURITY

Here I am at our open door awaiting
your words to full this space . . .

Today we will speak of purity. This word conjures up a host of
meanings in your world. But our direction today is not to focus
on the cleanness in the meaning of the word; our focus is on
the spirit of the word as it was used in creation. Let us try to
do this by contrasting the ways your world uses the word and
the meaning we see in the word. Many groups in your world
use this word as a way to exclude others, as in, keeping the
bloodlines in a race of people pure or keeping an idea pure
and ignoring any perceived contamination by any addition or
improvement to that idea. This is not the purity we speak of;
our Purity is all inclusive and all encompassing. It is the purity
that allowed for the creation of mankind. It is the pinpoint
focus of the most essential creative energy that became man. It
is the Purity of the ONE whose loving energy created all that
you see and all that you are. This Purity knows no bounds and
excludes nothing. This purity brought all colors into being,
just as all the colors of your world encase the same miracle of
life. You can't remove the color of a person's skin and expect to
find a different interior from your own. All humanity contains
the same miracles of life. The outer covering is just a choice,
a way to walk through your world. No different than choosing
a bicycle, a car, or a plane in which to travel. But in all the
millennia that man has existed, this visual contrast still evokes
dissention in some. It causes wars, death, destruction and
atrocities simply because of a misguided belief in what some of
you describe as purity. Please consider what we say here seriously
for Purity is the basic truth of all that exists in your world.

RESURRECTION

Here I am at our open door awaiting
your words to fill this space . . .

Resurrection seems to be an appropriate topic for today,
since today is a celebration of one of your greatest teachers.
The resurrection story is one that is played out in each of
your lives every new day you awaken to your world. It is a
promise of a new start, a day you have been given to walk
your life path making any choices or changes you wish.
There is no greater gift than the gift of another day.

An Invitation

Here I am at our open door awaiting
your words to fill this space . . .

You will note that when you sit to work here with us on these
pages, the pain you have felt in your back disappears. (Our
gift to you?)—No, it is your gift to yourself. Your consciousness
shifts when you sit to do this work, and your body responds to
that shift by recognizing that your body is in perfect health
when your mind is soul-centered. This is a concept that is
very difficult for humans to grasp, because you must live so
fully in your physical world and shifting to experience a soul
consciousness means letting go of all the attachments to your
physical world for a while. This concept does not have a strong
attraction in your world. You are trained almost from birth to
want to grasp and control the world around you, so letting go
of it willingly, even for a small amount of time, is unthinkable.
But there are so many advantages to learning to shift your
consciousness, which is one of the many reasons for these pages.
We have spoken of meditation, we have spoken of finding a
place of peace in each of your days in which to get quiet and
find your soul center, and we have spoken of trying your hand
at stepping back from the dramas in your life and the lives
around you so that you can see with your soul's eye what is really
taking place. Each of these practices can help you experience
that shift in consciousness we speak of because each of these
activities, when mastered, broadens your vision and hones your
perceptions. We sincerely hope that you will give each of these
activities a try and give your life the lift that the experience
will provide. We wish you each the wonder of the adventure of
learning about an aspect of yourself that you have yet to meet.

EYES

*Here I am at our open door awaiting
your words to fill this space . . .*

We have said that there is no greater gift than the gift of
another day. Yet you look at the same new day and see just that,
sameness. All of these pages are trying very sincerely to tell you
that you must use your soul's eyes to see "every day" life. With
these eyes you can see the true purpose, the true reality, and
the true pattern and path that you have set for yourself. With
these eyes the people around you become messengers to give
you clues to your next step, not drama filled players blocking
your journey through life. With these eyes you can discern the
truth of every situation and stand back from the conflagration
of energy that pollutes the senses and mask the intention of
the participants. We have repeatedly asked that you take the
time to search your inner self and find the consciousness that
will allow you to use these eyes to walk through your world. We
will continue to do so because without them your life path can
become drudgery and a trial from which you see no escape. This
mind set will blind you to the adventures and possibilities that
surround you every day. Don't bury yourself in the sameness
of your days when it is relatively easy to access new eyes and
see the light of possibilities in each encounter, in each new
dawn and in each waking moment. Please take the time to
learn to enrich your lives. We are always walking with you.

YOUR PRECIOUS BODY

Here I am at our open door awaiting
your words to fill this space . . .

Your body is the vehicle which you have chosen for your journey.
The majority of you rarely give it a thought as long as it is
functioning properly. But your body, in and of itself, is a living
miracle. Not only because of the millions of separate but distinct
functions it completes every second of every day, but because
every atom of it is imbued with life's essential energy. You race
around in your world day after precious day and complete your
tasks, stay connected with family and friends, go to work and
never give a thought to the vehicle that makes all of this frenzied
movement possible. Then you wonder why the body breaks down
occasionally. As some of you have come to realize, the body
breaks down, in one way or another, when you don't pay attention
to the little hints it is giving you to stop and rest, or reevaluate.
Your body will stop you when you ignore its more subtle signals
and keep going as you always do without checking in on how you
really feel, and listening to what it has to say. We would suggest
here a simple daily check-in with your body. Why not check in
with it each morning when brushing your teeth? You look in the
mirror, you brush your teeth, and you, seriously thank your body
for all it does for you. Does this sound strange or stupid to you?
It isn't! Gratitude is one of the greatest gifts you can bestow, so
why not be grateful to the vehicle that propels you through your
life? Energize your body each morning by acknowledging the role
it plays in your life; thank it for its support, its strength and its
endurance, and pay attention to its response. If something is not
right with your body you will know, the sooner the better, and take
heed to supply whatever is needed. Your life can only be improved
by this momentary focus on the miracle that encases your soul.

INFLUENCE

Here I am at our open door awaiting
your words to fill this space . . .

Today's topic is influence. We want to touch on the messages
both overt and covert that influence you and your choices in
your daily life. We are sure that many of you are aware that
your surroundings influence, to a great extent, the choices
you make, the way you behave and your mental state. Your
places of business, whether it is a restaurant, a department
store, or a church, certainly are aware that the surroundings
can influence your mind and heart. What about your home?
What about your own room? Pictures on the wall, books on
the shelf, even the colors you surround yourself with all add up
to influence you in one way or another. So we would suggest
that you take a good look around you, see everything anew,
with those soul's eyes, and read the story of the influence it is
having in your life. The majority of these influential messages
are subliminal, but they are very effective, and when combined
with the energy signature in a home or business or church,
they can have a very strong message. Bright colors can call to
the creative side of you which is great because it can open up
an area of your life that may have been ignored. But blend
those bright colors with an energy that is hostile or grating
and it creates a discordant atmosphere that can promote anger
and dissention. There are many less than positive marriages
of energy and décor that effect humans without them being
consciously aware of if, so we ask that you train yourself to be
alert to your surroundings wherever you are because you are
the only one who can choose where you go, who you are with,
and what you put in your home. All of these choices have great
impact on your day to day living. If we asked you to create a

space in your imagination where you could go to be at peace and happy, what would you create? Be aware of your response, it is never the same for any two people. You are unique and your needs on a physical and energetic level are unique. You are also the only one who can know what is restful or peaceful to you. So be aware and create your surroundings accordingly. Doing so will feed your soul and nurture your body, mind and heart.

BEGINNINGS

Here I am at our open door awaiting
your words to fill this space . . .

Beginnings are wonderful things. The slate is clear, the world
awaits and anything is possible. Just as the beginning of married
life with "William and Katherine" is pure, precious and an
event to rejoice in; so is a new beginning in any of your lives.
That new beginning can start at any time. Making a choice
to start your life anew is one of the most powerful gifts you
are given in human form. We don't mean making a massive
change in your life like moving to a different part of your
world and beginning your life over again from nothing. We
are addressing the issue of experiencing your life as it exists
right now with a new set of eyes and emotional filters. Just as
impaired eyesight can be improved with new glasses, so your life
can be improved with new perceptions. Only you can make the
choice to put the effort into reaching for those new perceptions,
but we can assure you that making the effort will make all
the difference in how you experience your life. Give yourself
the opportunity to see your life as it exists on a soul level by
following the suggestions we have laid out in these pages. We
can assure you that you will be amazed at the adventures that
await you and the knowledge that will make clear your path.

HEALTH

Here I am at our open door awaiting
your words to fill this space . . .

Death of the physical body does not mean the passing out
of existence of the Soul. Though there are many in your
world that have no belief in the Soul, that disbelief does
not negate the fact that souls exist. Your soul is the essence
that infuses the physical body, and the soul's energy is the
battery that powers it. That energy can be found in every
atom of your human body. This is not something that is
taken into consideration by humans, especially in your
medical communities, but it is a fact none the less.

Starting from this premise let us suppose that the body is ill.
What you will see as the cause of that illness will be dependent
on what you see as the symptoms. However, in our realm we
know that illness in the body is, generally, simply a physical
manifestation of energy that has been polluted or misused for
a long period of time. So essentially, illness is derived from your
environment, your actions, your words and your thoughts. This
is not a new idea it has been around in your world for centuries.
It is obviously not an idea that garners a lot of attention
however. We have spoken in these pages about energy before,
about how essential it is to learn to keep your energy clean,
about how important it is to surround yourself with compatible
ideas, visual stimuli, books, colors, and people who enrich and
enhance your life. All of these are meant as a prescription, if
you will, for good physical health. The more you are steeped
in drama, chaos, or any of the host of other negative emotions
or environments the more you risk your physical health. We
also realize that it is next to impossible to avoid all negativity

in your world. This is why we recommend that you cleanse your own energy on a daily basis, perhaps making it a part of your nighttime routine. This is not time consuming at all, it can be as easy as closing your eyes and envisioning your energetic body in your mind, then simply flushing the toilet! Everyone knows what that sounds like, so it should be easy to do this little exercise anywhere. As you flush the toilet mentally see all the polluting energy you have picked up during the day flush out of your body and down a drain; simple and effective. This is a very easy way to help your physical body stay clean and healthy.

BALANCE

Here I am at our open door awaiting
your words to full this space . . .

Balance is our topic today. We would ask that you mentally
go through your day and remember all the events that ate up
the hours. Was it made up of work and chores and hurry and
worry and electronic connectivity to your world? Did it entail
driving and buying and picking up and delivering and doing
all manner of things that needed to be fit into a time schedule?
Did it include time for you, just you, to stop and breathe
and see your world? Did it include time for you to enjoy your
physical body? Did it include time to close your eyes and hear
the sounds of nature in an environment that allowed those
sounds to be heard? Think about this carefully. If there is no
balance of work and appreciation in your life it is like trying
to ride a bicycle with only one tire, you can't help but fall
over. Some of you diehards out there will say people can ride
unicycles, all it takes is learning to balance on one wheel. Yes,
that is very true, but then all of your attention is on keeping an
unnatural balance, and none of it is left for you. Is that really
how you honestly want to live your life? As in all other things,
the choice is yours. But on the side of balance, it can add
freedom, relaxation and calm perspective to your life. All of
these things can make your life longer, healthier, happier and
less stressful. How, when and what you choose to incorporate
into your life is up to you and only you. Please choose wisely.

FIND YOUR DRIVE

Here I am at our open door awaiting
your words to fill this space . . .

Each of you has a drive inherent in your choice of this life
path. That drive, that purpose is often buried under all the
layers of everyday living. We would encourage you to start
looking for the passion that energized your soul to create and
initiate this life you are living. If there was not a strong reason
for you to have chosen to be in human form you would not be
in human form. So find your passion and let it guide you to
where your heart and soul need you to go. The direction of
your life, your commitment to it and your focus on it are your
purpose for being. So many of you lose sight of this or never
even give it a passing thought. But it is true for each and every
person. Finding the magnet that pulls at your spirit, your mind,
and your heart is the greatest thing you can do for yourself
and your world. You came here to do and be something more
than you may currently be expressing. Find the drive that will
propel you into the life you were meant to live and give it your
focus and your energy. We are here to assist, to encourage
and to cheer for you. Choose to live a passion filled life doing
whatever it was that drew you to your world, and watch the
energy around you change into a revitalization of your life.

A DIFFICULT PATH

Here I am at our open door awaiting
your words to fill this space . . .

The "open door" you have chosen as the theme for these pages
is more than just a metaphor. We enjoy hearing your statement
of intention each time you sit down to transcribe these pages.
Opening that door and waiting there for the information to
be passed through shows us the focused free will choice you
have made to do this work. The fact that you return each day
to continue this journey is a reinforcement of that choice. We
have stated before that each day is a new beginning, a chance
for new choices and changes in your lives. We are very grateful
that each day you choose to continue this journey with us. Each
of you makes similar choices every day to continue your lives
without making changes or to make changes and take your
lives in new directions. It amazes us that most of these choices
are made without conscious or focused thought. We encourage
each of you to dissect your day and be aware of the conscious
and unconscious choices you make over and over again. Look
closely at each of them and make sure they bring meaning and
clarity to your life. Becoming aware of these choices is essential
if you wish to be the master of your life; being the master of
your life means that you take control of your thoughts, your
words and your actions. Once you have taken that step you hold
the total responsibility for all you think, say and do. No one
else can ever be blamed for what happens on your life path.
Perhaps that is why this is a difficult path for humans to choose.

OUTLOOK

Here I am at our open door awaiting
your words to fill this space . . .

Outlook is the topic for today. The word is interesting to us. It
is the out picturing of what is happening inside you. So your
outlook is really a manifestation of your internal condition.
The way you see your world is dependent upon what is going
on inside you. This is not true of everyone in your world, but
for the vast majority it is accurate. We wonder why it is so
difficult for you to see that you project onto the outside world
the self-talk, attitude and energy that permeate your internal
universe. You do have an internal universe, you know, one that
only you control. You accept or reject ideas, attitudes, thought
patterns, and emotions; you choose to incorporate them into
your life or not. You set up your pattern for living and this
gives you your outlook. That outlook adds your own imprint
of energy onto your world. Think about that for a minute.
Your energy imprint added to the billions of other energy
imprints worldwide works to set up your global energy. Put in
plain language this way it really makes the masses of humanity
responsible for all of the chaotic energy that is whipping
around your planet. You can say you are only one person so
that can't make that much difference. But you can only start
with what you control, and that is you. If you don't like what is
happening in your world start with what you control. Change
your internal universe before you try to affect your external
world. You have control over this choice and we encourage
you to put your energy into some internal spring cleaning.

SURROUNDINGS

Here I am at our open door awaiting
your words to fill this space . . .

Do you find peace in your surroundings? Do you find comfort in
your surroundings? Do you find strength in your surroundings?
If the answer to any of these questions is no, why are you there?
Why are you choosing to inhabit a space that gives you no peace,
comfort or strength? In answering this question you should be
able to tell a great deal about the priorities in your life. If your
answer is because of other people in your life, then we ask that
you please examine what these other people mean to you and
why you are allowing them to hold you in a space that is not
nurturing to you. If your answer is financial, then we still ask
why there is no peace, comfort, or strength. Finances or lack
thereof don't make a place peaceful, comfortable or nurturing,
your own mindset can do that. If you live in a non-nurturing
space try to figure out why. Most people who live in such spaces
are getting something out of being there. Only you can say
what that something is. We realize it is a difficult thing to do.
Assessing your surroundings in this way is uncomfortable and
may bring up a lot of questions you don't wish to address. If
that is the case ignore this message and move on to the next
message. When the time is right for you to address this issue you
can come back here and do that. There are times when walking
your life path means you are deliberately in uncomfortable
surroundings in order to learn or teach a valuable lesson. So just
make a simple assessment and if you do not wish to delve into
the questions posed here do not concern yourself. The time will
come when you will eagerly come back to this page and reassess
your surroundings. Until then remember there are those who
walk with you to be supportive in all the passages of your life.

SPEAKING

Here I am at our open door awaiting
your words to fill this space . . .

We have often talked about energy in these pages, but do you realize that each word you speak has both the energy you instill in it and the energy inherent in the meaning of the word? This is very true. So imagine all the energy you are expelling every time you speak! With this in mind will you now pause before you speak and remember the energy that is a passenger on your words? The reason all the positive words in your language light you up and make you happy isn't just because of the meaning of the word, it's because of the energy added to it by the speaker. The same thing applies to the negative words that can make you feel dark, depressed, and desperate. This is the reason people are either enthralled or repelled by public speakers. The best of these people rise to high office in your world because the message they convey is one that resonates at an energetic level with the masses. This is a powerful gift and using it to enrich, encourage and enlighten is one of the best ways to enliven the world that surrounds you. Find the positive in each person and situation and speak that truth. This is the easiest and most available tool you have to change the world around you. Choose to speak light instead of dark, choose to speak encouragement instead of condemnation, choose to speak ideas instead of judgments and watch as you create a world of difference in your surroundings.

PASSAGES

Here I am at our open door awaiting
your words to fill this space . . .

There are passages or sections in each life path that necessitate
a slowing down or pausing of life's normal activities in order
to give your spiritual and energetic aspects time to shift into
a new mental and emotional framework. These passages can
include feelings of wanting to be away from family and friends,
of disinterest in many things that were essential previously, of
feeling tired, anxious and somewhat disoriented. We would like
to assure you that each soul in human form experiences these
passages. Some to a greater degree than others but all humans
do experience them. The souls that find themselves deeply
embedded in these passages are the souls with the biggest
changes on the horizon. When life paths shift it is because that
is the way you organized your life before you took your first
breath, so our encouragement would be to take a deep breath
and allow your soul to guide your transition into the next
phase of your life. Everywhere you turn in your world you see
humans struggling with these transitional or passage periods
of their lives. If we can convince you of one thing please let it
be that you planned well, and that it is OK to trust your soul
to guide you through this life. Also to remember that you have
an energetic team that walks with you, souls that are dedicated
to the successful completion of the life you set out for yourself.
Don't forget to ask for help from them, for there are many times
when they can help you find the calm in the eye of the storm.

Honoring

Here I am at our open door awaiting
your words to fill this space . . .

Today you celebrate the role of mothers. We would choose
to use the word "honoring" rather than celebrating. For us
it conveys more of the sense of appreciation rather than the
sense of partying. Honoring someone for the role they have
undertaken in their life is far more of a tribute than throwing
a party to celebrate them. Honoring them means standing
up to give testimony to the impact they have had on your
life, it means setting your own life aside for a small space of
time and focusing on the dedication, energy and drive that
someone else showed you which set an example for you or
enriched your life. This form of honoring is not very prevalent
in your world except at memorial services. This is a practice
we would encourage you to change. Honoring someone,
showing appreciation to them and expressing gratitude for
their presence in your life enriches, clarifies and binds the
souls involved. It creates clear and concise communication
from the heart. It feeds the souls of all who are present.
Acknowledging these gifts of spirit seems to make many of
you very uncomfortable. This is something which has been
difficult for us to understand. Perhaps because of the way you
use your energy in your world it is easier to celebrate than to
honor. Celebrating is, as we said, more like a party. You are
familiar with the energy expended in a party atmosphere, so
it is easier. At a party you show up in your finery and present
your best self for all to see. Expending energy in an honoring
manner is entirely different; it is calling upon your heart and
soul to speak instead of your ego. In honoring someone else
you sublimate yourself and give credit and accolade from

your soul to another soul. The truest of friendships engage in honoring regularly, because it is a true blending of hearts and souls. This is a rare and precious gift in your world. How many of these relationships do you have in your life?

OPPORTUNITY/GIFTS

Here I am at our open door awaiting
your words to fill this space . . .

Do you realize that each day you are given an opportunity to
change your life? Most of these are opportunities for small
changes, but sometimes a big one pops up. The big ones are
rarely missed but the small ones are rarely even noticed. It
could be a conversational opportunity with someone you
speak with a lot, it could be a stranger looking lost, it could
be an animal needing help, it could be a homeless person
whose eyes you won't meet. All of these and many more are
"opportunity moments in time" that can give you an insightful
look into your life and the lives around you. More often than
not each of you is so caught up in your own web of need,
want, must do, schedule, errands, chores and work that you
are unaware of your immediate surroundings. We are not
asking you to stop your world and make massive changes,
because your world is what you have made it for a very good
reason. However, we do encourage you to check in once or
twice a day to the <u>real</u> reality of life, the reality of soul to soul
communication. We are aware that this is beginning to sound
very repetitive, but that does not make it any less important.
The cause, the reason and the reality of your existence on
earth was your choice and your plan. So be aware that what
surrounds you is there because you put it there. Be aware
that it all has some gift to give you, even if that gift is just the
realization that you no longer need it in your world. So many
of you take all the people you have ever known your whole
life along on this lifetime ride, when if you stopped to pay
attention you would realize that the gift they gave to your life
was given long ago and your paths now need to diverge. This

is not losing a friend, this is allowing life to move on, allowing life to flow freely, and allowing space for more timely gifts to flow into your life. Give your life the gift of looking closely at it with your soul's eyes wide open and see what you find.

THE PATH HOME

*Here I am at our open door awaiting
your words to fill this space . . .*

You think of your "Creation Diety" as the One who gives life,
and the initial spark of life certainly originated from that
Omnipotent Power. But as we have said before, you made the
choices, you assembled the cast of characters, and you wrote the
outlines of the script for this particular life. You did it with the
encouragement of, and in harmony with, a group of souls whose
role it is to be the "nurturers" of new lives. This is why they are
committed to being available to you. This idea is not new in your
world. It is not that much different than Catholics praying to
a variety of "saints" when they are in need of assistance. Many
of your organized religions promote the same idea of having a
group of celestial beings ready to listen to your pleas for help.
The reality is that you have a group that is all your own, made
up of souls who have interacted with you over millennia, always
with the same goal. That goal is to assist each other in attaining
our reunion with that Omnipotent Power. Thus this fascinating
world of Earth with all of its challenges and distractions
becomes the Universal Olympics. This place where souls come
to hone their skills in seeing past the obvious, in identifying
the underlying energy, in finding their driving purpose, in
becoming the out picturing of what their soul meant them to be
in this particular existence. Just as you admire those who attain
the Medals in your earthly Olympics, so should you admire
those who have the strength of purpose and grace of character
in the Olympics of the Soul. You know who these people are, you
have seen them or been touched by them in one way or another
throughout your life. They are the people who transcend
the artificial barriers your world builds simply because they

refuse to acknowledge the existence of those barriers. They do not see color, race, wealth, poverty, or species as barriers because ALL LIFE is precious to them. All life contains a miraculous spark of the Omnipotent Power called the soul.

We understand that what we have said here can cause disbelief, confusion, and argument. But beneath any angst you may feel about this information, can you also feel the possibility of truth? Can you look beneath the emotion and feel the reality? This is what we encourage you to do: to look beneath your earthly programming and find your souls' path Home.

NATURE

Here I am at our open door awaiting
your words to fill this space . . .

Natural settings on your earth if left untouched are places of
peace, beauty and natural rhythms that feed the soul. Even
the parks you manufacture inside your cities can replicate
that sense of peace if you tune in closely enough. That
natural rhythm feeds all the parts and places of the human
being as well. Getting out into nature is as important to your
complete health as breathing the air. Do you feel that is an
overstatement? It isn't, just consider that each encounter in
your day contains energy that is at the very least different than
your own, and at the very worst abrasive and harmful. With
each of these encounters your energetic body is impacted
to some extent. So how do you alleviate the stress of these
encounters and cleanse your energetic self? As we have said
before there are visual practices which can help to reset the
balance of your energy, but one of the best and most effective
ways is to immerse yourself in a natural setting and breathe
in the natural balance of natures' energy. Giving yourself this
gift goes a long way to keeping your stress levels down and
your mental balance stable. Giving yourself this gift also takes
the pressure off the other relationships in your life because it
adds the ability to see with loving eyes situations which if seen
through chaotic energy might cause friction. Giving yourself
some time in nature enriches not only your life but the lives
around you. Find yourself a spot in your immediate world
where you can go to shed the angst and stress of your day or
your week and take advantage of natures' ability to heal.

YOUR WORLD

Here I am at our open door awaiting
your words to fill this space . . .

Your world has a tendency to ascribe qualities of right
or wrong, good or bad, helpful or hurtful to each of the
situations or occurrences in your lives or your world in
general. In our world this is not so. Here something either is
or is not, no judgment is placed as to whether being or not
being is good or bad. Whatever is; simply is. The only interest
we all have in equal measure is the interest in returning
to our source; in becoming one again with all that is. For
the majority of souls in human form this concept is well
beyond your ability to fathom. We give you this information
simply to bring it into your realm of conscious thought. We
are aware that there are others who have shared this basic
truth with your world, and that there are pockets of spiritual
intensity in your world where this truth is contemplated
with great energy and a driven style of life that promotes
this ideal. We are also aware that these areas of your world
are very rare. We are not trying to make your whole world
into mirror images of those idyllic places. Your world is as
it is because it has a purpose in being that way. Billions of
souls have chosen to be there, each for a specific reason.
It is very daunting when you really stop to think about it.
Each soul with its own purpose, not knowing the purpose
driving every other soul it meets. And yet in all of this
seeming confusion there is a grand design, a road, or life
path for each soul which allows them to meet those souls
necessary to move forward with their purpose at just the
right time and place, and all of this was orchestrated by each
individual soul before you drew your first breath. Now that is

miraculous. So your world is a place of miraculously driven souls who have taken human form for a purpose. Wouldn't it be amazing if all of you realized that and could look at each other with that information at the forefront of your minds?

KNOWLEDGE

Here I am at our open door awaiting
your words to fill this space . . .

The human mind in the framework of its' full evolution is very young. So the knowledge you yearn for is almost exclusively the knowledge obtained from experience, from books and from your educational institutions. But there is another kind of knowing, one that each and every one of you has experienced at least once along your life path. That is the knowing of something that cannot be seen, heard or experienced but is known in the heart or the spirit. You have sometimes called this an "Ah-hah moment", or intuition but what is really happening is that you are touching your soul self, the part of you that is a part of the spark of creation. In that connection the reality of any situation becomes blindingly clear. Some of you have many of these moments, others have very few, and the difference in the frequency of these moments is the difference in the mindset of the individual. If, in your conscious mind, you can allow that there is a greater power to which you can link so that you can experience the clarity of any given situation then you will be willing to use that connection more often in your life. If this concept is strange to you or difficult to grasp then you will rarely experience this connection. What we wish to impress upon you is that your life path runs so much more smoothly when you can accept this premise and surrender your need for empirical knowledge and shift your consciousness to a higher realm so that you may benefit from the knowledge your soul seeded into the soil of your life. Tending to this internal garden of knowledge can allow you to reap a harvest of truth, vision and instincts that will wrap your life experience in an amazing layer of miraculous events. As in all things in your human realm this too is your choice.

YOUR PURPOSE

Here I am at our open door awaiting
your words to fill this space . . .

We are returning to the idea of Purpose in your life. What
fascinates you, what draws your attention and interest, what
particular thing lights you up inside, what are you good at,
what is easy for you to do? The answers to these questions can
bring you very close to understanding what your purpose is,
because the things you have an affinity for are the stepping
stones on the pathway to your purpose for this life you are
living. It is so easy for a soul in human form to become stuck
in doing something that is dull and boring to them just so
they can "make a living". But please try to remember that
you are not on earth just to "make a living". There really is a
purpose for you to be there . . . really! Finding that purpose is
a major step in making a success of this life path you created.
We don't know how many different ways we can convey this
message, and we are in earnest about making sure we make
this point. Find your purpose and your path will clear. Find
your purpose and the trivialities that weigh on you daily will
lighten. Find your purpose and the irritants of your life will
fade when they are no longer your focus. Because finding your
purpose means the greatest measure of your energy will now be
focused on what you came into this life to accomplish, and that
will bring you joy and peace in a way nothing else ever can.

YOUR COMPANIONS

Here I am at our open door awaiting
your words to fill this space . . .

We have spoken before of the number of tools you have at your
disposal to accompany you on this life path you have chosen.
Using your soul's eyes to view situations in your life, getting in
touch with your inner knowledge, using visualization to keep
your energy clean and meditation to clear your mind can all
help you to stay steady and focused on your life path. Also
acknowledging that there are those energies that are committed
to walking this life path with you is another tool. We have said
before and will continue to stress that each of the energies
that are dedicated to seeing you succeed in this life you have
chosen are there to be your unseen companions in this journey.
Oftentimes the life path chosen is one in which there will be
little or no connection to this realm and those energies that
choose to accompany that soul will do so knowing they can
only be a silent blessing. To you that may sound like a useless
waste, but to us it is a measure of the honor we have for each
other. Knowing there is very little chance of connection to the
soul we travel with does not negate the honor that is bestowed
when we are asked to, and agree to travel with that soul.
Everything here is done in harmony. Your world is the world
where clashes of ego, discontent, envy, anger, and all of the
negative emotions can be played out to teach or to learn all that
is necessary to return to our Source. In harmony and purpose
you choose your life and the silent companions who walk with
you, in harmony and purpose those companions agreed to
honor your choice and stand with you while you walk that
chosen path. That is the strength of this commitment we have
to each other, this honoring of all that you are and are striving

to become, and all that we are and are striving to become. This is the journey all souls take, as many times as necessary, as many different ways as necessary, whether in body or in energy, we travel this road together on our pilgrimage Home.

Clearing Your Path

Here I am at our open door awaiting
your words to fill this space . . .

Today is a blank page in the book of this life you have chosen.
Can you choose to make it better than yesterday? Can you
choose to eliminate just one of those attitudes, habits, irritants
that prevent your life path from proceeding more smoothly? If
you can, if you choose to, then you will have opened a door to
your inner self, your soul and to those who walk with you. It is
most difficult to walk your chosen life path when it is hidden by
all the attitudes, energy, and habits that create obstacles along
the way. It is like navigating through a minefield. You never
know when something is going to blow up on you. But take just
one of these encumbrances that weigh you down and set it aside,
remove it from your path and the way becomes so much easier,
so much clearer. Can you think of one thing you can set aside?
Just one thing that really isn't who you are, but which you use to
express yourself or to protect yourself? Can you set aside that
habit or attitude? If you can, and you can eliminate it from your
life, you can choose again and eliminate something else which
doesn't reflect who you are. Eventually there will only be the
you that was meant to be walking this life path, the soul which
came into being through the love of our Creator, the soul who
chose to be on your earth at this time for a very specific reason.
You and the energies who accompany you, free to pursue the
purpose you set out to accomplish this lifetime. Isn't it about
time to clear your path, to open your door and move forward?

DIFFICULT TRANSITIONS

Here I am at our open door awaiting
your words to fill this space . . .

Each life path contains transitional periods. These are
more frequent in some lives than in others. If an especially
challenging life path is chosen it is likely that there will be more
transitional periods, simply because staying on a path that is laid
out with many obstacles is difficult. So the human body driving
the soul decides to veer from the path. This is not unusual and
is to be expected. Choosing a less stressful path for a while is a
normal and natural response to this kind of life path. But for
those souls who chose a difficult life path and have traveled
it with grace, fortitude and focus there is a different kind of
transition period. This is probably the more difficult transition
though it doesn't sound like it to the human ear. This is the
transition of letting go. This is the transition of understanding
that the hard work is done, the foundation has been laid, the
house has been built, and all the tasks have been completed.
Now it is time to change from the attitudes of the laborer and
accept that what you have done is good work and move into the
release of a different aspect of your soul self that will now be
charged with finishing this journey. This transition is so much
more difficult because it requires that the soul who has held
on to its life path so steadfastly and diligently now release the
reins to a part of itself that it has not had a strong connection
with for a long time. Learning to trust this new aspect of self
even when there is a strong instinctual knowledge that it is the
right thing to do is very difficult. Getting caught up in the very
strong drug of working so hard that there is nothing left in your
life but a few grains of lightness is what happens in these very
difficult lifetimes. Being so driven to prove that you can achieve

what you set out to do no matter what the obstacle becomes so much a part of what you are that it takes great strength to let it go and accept that that particular part of the job is done. For these souls we watch and encourage and keep faith even though in their struggle with this change they cannot feel us.

EMULATE YOUR HEROES

Here I am at our open door awaiting
you words to fill this space . . .

In the past century in your world there have been souls who have had the tenacity of spirit to grab their purpose and hone it with a razor sharp focus that changed the perceptions and perspectives of millions of people worldwide. You know their names because they have become a part of your past history: Mahatma Ghandi, Mother Teresa, Nelson Mandela to name just a few. There are also the souls who are currently using the technologies of your world to reach many more millions with messages of hope, help, harmony, humor and happiness. The most visible of these is Oprah Winfrey. These people have found their purpose and harnessed all of their energy, belief and passion to it and brought their vision to the world at large. You look at these people in amazement and then look at your own life and think it is too small to make any difference, but you couldn't be more wrong. For all of the amazing inroads in the apathy of the human condition that these larger than life souls have accomplished they are each just one soul, just as you are. Yes, they have gathered to them like minded souls who have helped them fulfill their vision on a grand scale, but that was and is their purpose. To wake up humanity and give it its booster shot of loving, honoring and compassion toward all those who inhabit your planet. Your role may be the microcosm to their macrocosm but you still have an important role to play right where you are. The people you touch every day are in your life for a reason. Look for that reason and honor it and them, all of them, with being present when you are with them. We mean really be present: bring the Ghandi, Mandela, Mother Teresa and Oprah part of your own soul into expression in every day of your life. You all have aspects of what these people have spent their lives expressing in your own soul. Find them. That's what each of the teachers who have walked your planet wanted you to do. Find that part of yourself that is the essential seed God put there and give birth to it in your life.

DREAMS

Here I am at our open door awaiting
your words to fill this space . . .

We have stated in past pages that we can only assist in your lives
when you allow us to do so. This can be done most effectively
through prayer because prayer hones your energy and focus.
However there are times when we communicate through your
dreams. These are times when we see paths you are taking or
situations in your life that you may be missing or unaware of
because your focus is elsewhere. In dreams we can use symbols
that have meaning for you to "wake you up" to what we see.
These dreams are most often the dreams you remember when
you awaken. If you take the time to write them down and
research the meanings of the symbols in them you will get a clue
to what we see happening in your life. We would suggest that
you find a dream book that is based in the spiritual meaning
of dreams. There are many available to you. Paying attention to
the dreams you remember is an excellent way to stay on track
with your life path. We can connect with you in this manner
without any prayer or request from you, because it is merely a
subtle nudge, if you will, and one that you, more often than
not, totally ignore. Sometimes dreams stay with you because
they scare you, or they are repetitive in nature. These really
are dreams that you will want to explore. They have important
information for you. We don't interfere on a whim; it has to
be important for us to do so. But as with all the crossroads on
your life path, it is up to you whether you will pay attention.

GRACE

Here I am at our open door awaiting
you words to fill this space . . .

How many people have brought Grace into your life? We ask
that you consider this question carefully. Grace is a quality that,
for us, brings the love, harmony, goodness and blessings of your
Creator into being in your world. Can you recall moments in
your life when someone has done this for you? You should all
be able to recall at least a time or two when this miracle has
happened to you. We say this because in planning your life path
you seed it with these moments of Grace. This is a soul to soul
contract. It allows for a momentary glimpse of what being in our
realm is like. For here there is honoring and understanding,
love and acceptance, joy and hope. The soul who agrees to
share moments of this Grace in your life is a messenger sent
to give you a reminder of who you are and what life is really
all about. This gift of Grace may be an anomaly of behavior
for the person giving the gift. That is to say that the giver may
not be a person whose normal human behavior would tend
toward spreading Grace in your world. However when a soul has
committed to another soul to be the bearer of Grace this pact
will supersede all other human programming and express itself
at the appointed time. This is one of the wonderful miracles of
planning a life path; it allows these glimpses into the Light even
when you are mired in your human life with all of its demands.
Be alert, and watch for these moments of Grace and remember
what a wise soul you were to plan to have them in your life.
Also remind yourself that the soul bringing that moment of
Grace to you honored your soul and theirs by doing so.

GENDER ENERGY

Here I am at our open door awaiting
your words to fill this space . . .

Have you ever pondered on the role you chose in this life you
are living? We don't mean the situational role; the gender role
is what we are asking about. It sounds as though that should be
very basic. You choose to be either male or female. But when
this choice is made you are choosing an energetic signature as
well, because the male and female energies are very different
and distinct. In bygone eras on your world there were very
few souls who changed this standard of balance. What we are
stating here is that for centuries women were enmeshed in
their female energy and men in their male energy. However
over the last century or so it has almost become the norm for
humans, regardless of their gender, to use whichever energy
suits the situation at hand. Women will switch to the more
assertive and brusque energy in situations where their normal
nurturing and understanding energy will not be useful. On the
other hand men will switch to the gentle, softer female energy
in situations where their normal strong and direct male energy
might be ineffective. This balancing of both streams of energy
has become the norm for the majority of your current societies.
It has had many benefits for the souls who have decided to
incorporate this blending of energies in their lives. It has
allowed men and women to step outside the stilted roles that
were once a given result of their gender. It has provided more
balanced societies in the areas of opportunities, ambitions,
expectations and possibilities. But like any major change in the
basic structure of a society this has been a double edged sword
for your world. It has taken many decades for this change to
be accepted as the norm, and still in some places around your

globe the old way prevails. Striving for equality and balance in all things is not for the meek of heart. It takes strong souls with a willingness to stand their ground and be heard. We want you to be aware of this basic activity in your daily life so that you can try to identify when people are switching the energy they are using. It really is very intriguing to watch and it will make you far more aware of the nuances in your surroundings.

LISTENING

Here I am at our open door awaiting
your words to fill this space . . .

Have you ever thought of listening as a gift? Listening, truly
listening to someone is a rare ability in your world. It isn't
that you don't have the ability to really listen it's just that you
don't make the effort to do it. There is so much more to be
gleaned from an interaction with others than you usually learn
simply because your inner attention is not really on the person
speaking with you, it is on how you will respond or what is
going on around you or your own inner conversation about
the current situation. If you train yourself to stop that inner
dialog and to ignore the outer visual stimulation which has
nothing to do with the communication at hand, you would be
amazed at what you can discern. As your psychologists have
discovered humans speak with more than their mouths. You
communicate on many levels and you don't need a degree to
begin to understand what is truly being communicated if you
will just hone your focus in on the person speaking with you.
Their gestures, body language, inflection, choice of words and
their facial expressions are some of the obvious indicators of
what they are trying to say, but underneath all of that is the
energetic identification of the communication. We have said
before that each of your words carries with it not only the
energy of the word but the energy you endow it with when you
give voice to it. We have asked you before in many of these
pages to learn to see with your souls' eyes the personal world
in which you live. We are now asking that you use your souls'
ears and perceptions to understand the true depth and width
of the communication you share with others. If you continue
as you have been you will continue to receive only part of what

is being conveyed to you. Like a bad cell phone connection you will only hear and understand pieces and parts of the message.

We simply ask that you try blocking out all other distractions and wholly invest yourselves in the conversations you have with others. We believe the difference you find will truly amaze you.

WHY? (PERSONAL)

Here I am at our open door awaiting
your words to fill this space . . .

On the wall in front of your computer desk is a replica of a portion of the "Creation of Adam" by Michelangelo. It depicts the section where the fingertips of God and Adam nearly touch. This image has held your attention and focus for many years. It has brought you great comfort and the inevitable question; Why? Why did Creation choose to express in this manner on your planet? One of your poets used the phrase "life's longing for itself", and that is probably the most accurate piece of truth for a human mind to understand. However, life isn't just what you recognize as life. It encompasses so much more, more than your eyes can see or your minds can comprehend. Your Earth and its Solar System are just one of the neighborhoods that are part of the Universal World. This topic is making you uncomfortable, but it is a seed of knowledge that needs to be planted here. Your planet is not alone in its beauty, vitality and life-supporting environment. We touched lightly on this information at the beginning of this journey with you. We want you to know that there is life and purpose elsewhere in the Universal World because just as one lone human being wouldn't last long or learn much, so too there is a need for other planetary environments for that learning and growth. Planets that support life (though perhaps not in a form you would readily recognize) are seeded throughout the Universal World. Planets that provide opportunities for souls to gather knowledge and experience on their road back to their Source. That is the ultimate purpose, to return to our Source after we have all completed our Universal Journey. There will never be a simplistic answer to the human's question "Why" when you are asking about your soul's journey or purpose. Our best advice is to go within and connect with who you are at a Soul level. When you do, you will begin to see and understand the larger purpose of your creation because a spark of your Creator is in each of you or you would not exist.

SUCCESSFUL JOURNEYS

Here I am at our open door awaiting
your words to fill this space . . .

The purpose of these pages is to give you information so that
you can more easily clear a space in your life to be who you
intended to be when you created this life path. We are not
referring to the roles you set for yourself or the relationship
roles you have taken on as you have walked your path; we are
talking about the expressing of who you are at a soul level. Your
journey along your life path is one thing, walking that path with
your soul in active attendance is a more in depth adventure.
The most successful journeys are a partnership between the
human form and the active participation, knowledge, and
awareness of your soul. When you can blend these two energy
forces into your life experience you have everything you need
to complete your journey successfully. The steps we have set
out in these pages are guidelines to use in achieving this goal.
We wish only to help make your journey all that your soul
wished it to be when it was conceived. It is all too easy to lose
track of what you wanted to accomplish when you are looking
at life through human eyes, and feeling the tugs and pulls
of life on your human body and mind. Take a moment and
ask yourself, "is this life I am living really why I am here?" If
the answer is "Yes" then ignore these pages, you don't need
them. But if the answer is "No", or you don't know the answer,
try rereading the pages that had special meaning for you.
Try stepping out of your habit patterns and adding a new
perspective to your life and see what doors it opens for you.

We wish you all a successful journey . . .

Final Page

Here I am at our open door awaiting
your words to fill this space . . .

This information has been couched in very simple terms, but
don't let the simplicity fool you. The most important truths
are very simple. Humans have a tendency to complicate very
simple truths. Time, for you, is linear so you must use it that
way; traveling forward on this journey of yours to reach your set
destination. We ask that you take whatever information you have
gleaned from these pages and implement it to lighten your load
and enhance your perceptions. Remember always the energies
that walk with you, you asked them to accompany you and
they made the commitment to do so. It is time for you to really
realize, at your soul's core, that you are not alone in your travels.
These pages are testimony to that Truth. Without collaboration
between both worlds they could not have been written. This type
of pipeline energy from our world to yours is not planned into
most life paths but that doesn't mean that the connection is any
less real. You have a strong group in each of your cultures that
believe in Angels who intervene, intercede, and protect. You call
them Angels we know them as the committed energies that walk
with each of you. We leave you with this pertinent prayer—

Angels be my guide today
See me safely on my way
By my side each step I pray
Till we come to the end of the day.